FACULTY
INVOLVEMENT
IN
LIBRARY
INSTRUCTION

LIBRARY ORIENTATION SERIES

edited by Sul H. Lee

Papers and summaries from the
Fifth Annual Conference on
Library Orientation for Academic Libraries
held at Eastern Michigan University,
May 15-17, 1975

FACULTY INVOLVEMENT IN LIBRARY INSTRUCTION

Their Views on Participation in and Support of
Academic Library Use Instruction

edited by
Hannelore B. Rader

Orientation Librarian
Eastern Michigan University

Published for the
Center of Educational Resources,
Eastern Michigan University
by

Pierian Press
ANN ARBOR, MICHIGAN
1976

Library of Congress Catalog Card No. 76-21914
ISBN 0- 87650-070-X

PIERIAN PRESS
P.O. Box 1808
Ann Arbor, Michigan 48106

Contents

Preface

The Fifth Annual Conference on Library Orientation for Academic Libraries was held May 15–17, 1975 at Eastern Michigan University, Ypsilanti, Michigan. This year's Conference was attended by one hundred and thirty-eight persons from thirty-one states and Canada.

The Conference dealt with "faculty involvement in library instruction" and covered the following topics: individual professors' views on library instruction; faculty reaction to a library-sponsored credit course on bibliographic instruction; faculty cooperation in a Council on Library Resources sponsored library instruction program; faculty involvement in an individualized approach to library instruction; and faculty cooperation in a library instruction program for graduate students. Panels, individual speakers, and group discussions were utilized to present these topics.

This publication contains, in order as presented, the speeches given during the Conference. However, questions and answers following the speeches and other discussions are not included.

One segment of the Conference entitled "Faculty Views on Library Instruction" is available in videocassette form from the ALA Headquarters Library in Chicago. The two-hour presentation, in color, may be obtained through inter-library loan.

The academic year 1974-75 was the final year of the five-year Library Outreach Orientation Program at Eastern Michigan University, funded jointly by the University, the Council on Library Resources (CLR), and the National Endowment for the Humanities (NEH). The Conferences, which were an outgrowth of the Library Outreach Orientation Program, were made possible because of the sponsorship of the CLR and NEH. This has been deeply appreciated by the staff of the Center of Educational Resources at Eastern Michigan University, as well as the many persons who have attended the five conferences at EMU.

We are pleased to report that the importance of academic library instruction has been recognized by EMU's faculty and administration, so that the University is providing full financial support for the continuation of the Library Outreach Orientation Program.

Recognition for contributions to the success of this year's Conference must be given to all the speakers and discussion group leaders who did an outstanding job in presenting their views and experiences in the area of library instruction. Special appreciation goes to Carolyn Kirkendall, Ann Andrew, and Laura Klann, members of the faculty and staff of the EMU Center of Educational Resources, for their support in planning and running this Conference.

Hannelore B. Rader

September 15, 1975

INTRODUCTION TO THE FIFTH ANNUAL CONFERENCE
on
LIBRARY ORIENTATION

Fred Blum

Director, Center of Educational Resources
Eastern Michigan University

It's a pleasure to welcome you to the Fifth Annual Conference on Library Orientation held at Eastern Michigan University.

I'm pleased to learn that we have one hundred and thirty-eight participants from thirty-one states and Canada. One hundred and nine institutions are represented. Once again, the Conference is in large part due to Hannelore Rader, our Orientation Librarian and Conference Coordinator. Those of you who know her will be glad to hear that her activities in this area have been recognized again, this time with a Council on Library Resources grant to identify and study ten successful library orientation programs and to write a guide for starting such programs.

Several other staff members have made indispensable contributions to our preparation for this conference. These include Mary Bolner, formerly Director of the Library Orientation Exchange (Project LOEX) and now a full-time Social Sciences Librarian; Carolyn Kirkendall, the present Director of Project LOEX; and Ann Andrew, Assistant Education and Psychology Librarian.

Several of our faculty, such as Professor Bertrand Ramsey of our Chemistry Department, are making vital contributions to the success of this Conference.

Off-campus participants, as you can see from your program, include specialists from the University of Michigan, University of Colorado, State University of New York at Syracuse, Texas A & M, Central Michigan University, and Earlham College.

Dean A.P. Marshall, who was Director of the Library at the inception of these conferences five years ago, deserves the thanks of all of us for his foresight in starting this noteworthy effort. It has become a catalyst for many other library orientation programs around the country.

I am personally grateful to Vice President James Magee for supporting my own effort to absorb the Library Orientation Program in our regular budget when the original five-year grant from the Council on Library Resources expires this September. The annual conferences are self-supporting, but the year-round effort to orient our students to the facilities, collections, services and use of the Center of Educational Resources is an instructional program which can only continue as long as faculty and administration agree that it is a necessary part of the educational process.

Actually, I think there's a common recognition that having a solid library orientation program is an "idea whose time has come." I use "orientation" in the broadest sense to include "Library Instruction." Everyone is interested in developments in this field. For example, when we made our own slide-tape library orientation program available through interlibrary loan, we quickly received 150 requests from about 40 states, Canada, and as far away as Israel.

From where I sit, library orientation is not only a necessary part of the educational process, but one of the top priority library programs -- on a par with collections development, reference service, and circulation as a *basic* library function. Indeed, it might be considered an integral part of reference service, except that while reference service is in large part a passive response to patron inquiry, library orientation is an aggressive reaching out to the student in the classroom, dormitory, student organization, or wherever else he may be found. Hence, the concept of "outreach-orientation."

This year's conference has as its theme a special aspect of that outreach, namely, reaching the student *through* the faculty member. This involves orienting faculty members to basic, as well as sophisticated, use of the library. I trust I will not offend any faculty members present when I say that there are probably few campuses in the country where over one-third of the faculty have an adequate understanding of the facilities, materials, and services available at their on-campus library. And only a minute fraction have any idea of the off-campus resources available free, or at nominal cost, *through* the library. Thus, teaching faculty frequently short-change their students by not themselves utilizing the most powerful instructional tool on campus.

Nobody on the teaching faculty need be offended by this observation, for it is the librarians' job to orient the faculty to optimum utilization of available resources and services, and in general they have only partially succeeded in this.

I think this has been due to a lack of well-defined systematic programs of faculty orientation. In some cases, librarians have lacked the talent or energy to pursue such programs; in others, teaching faculty have been reluctant to admit that they might learn something from librarians. And frequently the money is simply not available to support what could be an expensive program, requiring specialized interaction between teaching faculty and librarians.

I believe *faculty* library orientation is also an "idea whose time has come." We will be making special efforts in that regard over the next few years and we hope to have some interesting results to report at future conferences.

Here at Eastern, where we have integrated the library, audio-visual, and television functions in a single Center of Educational Resources, the scope of such a faculty orientation program would have to be a broad one, encompassing the full utilization of on-campus and off-campus resources in all of these areas.

Now, you may be saying to yourself, "Fine, I agree. We should have a systematic library orientation program, and one which includes the faculty. But how can we convince our library director and/or university administration to give us the money we need to undertake such a program?"

As you know, in this year of recession and double-digit inflation, a budget crunch has affected libraries all over the country. Therefore, I have asked various librarians, faculty, administrators, and outsiders, "Where can we find the money to expand our library orientation program?"

The responses have been informative, but not necessarily practical, since each suggestion involved trimming somebody else's program. For example:

The catalogers suggested cutting back reference service to four hours a day and acquiring less books.

One of the reference librarians suggested replacing the catalogers with students paid at the minimum wage.

A student assistant, when asked about this, approved of the concept, but suggested students should unionize and demand the same wage for the same work.

The unionized clerical workers thought the student assistants should be replaced by full-time clerical workers who, after all, would be around long enough to learn their jobs before graduating and, in any case, would not quit at peak load time to study for exams.

One member of the legislature couldn't understand why we didn't operate the library entirely on work-study, especially since this money comes from the Federal government.

Eight academic department heads suggested closing the library and apportioning its collections among the eight departments. They thought that the departmental secretaries could surely service these collections in addition to their other duties!

I, myself, suggested that probably the biggest saving could be made by giving each student an appropriate reading list for all of his courses and pointing him toward the library. He could then be guided in the use of the library by Hannelore Rader. His reading lists could be updated from time to time by our subject bibliographers. Reference librarians would assist him with any problems. Thus, teaching faculty would only need to develop curriculum, advise students, and grade periodic exams on the readings. This would result in a 72.895% reduction in faculty. In addition to the direct savings from this reduction, think of all the money that would be saved by the corresponding reduction in committee meetings, not to mention clerical and administrative support staff!

Unfortunately, upon hearing of this suggestion, the faculty voted to replace the library director with a tenured English professor, whose course had recently been eliminated for lack of students.

Now, if that digression tells us anything, it's that most of us are already running very tight ships. Money and staff to support orientation programs cannot be found by trimming other programs.

Therefore, new money must be found. To this end I would advise:

Draw up a good written proposal for your program, specifying why such a program is needed, the goals and objectives of the program, and what other institutions are doing in this area.

Indicate staff and other support needed and quantify this in dollars.

Get the support of your appropriate library committees and staff organization by working closely with them in developing your proposal.

Use your library newsletter and press releases in your college newspaper to reach your faculty and administration with word about your program and what you'll need to do the job. Be sure to tell them what other institutions are doing, especially the institutions that might be regarded as your competitors in recruiting students.

Get the full support of your library director. Ask him to accompany you on a carefully planned visit to an institution with a strong program in this field. Urge him to invite someone active in library orientation to your campus to discuss such programs with your staff. Call his attention to some of the relevant literature. As a last resort, you may have to undertake portions of the program on your own time as a practical demonstration of its value.

Let your director carry the ball in presenting the proposal to your faculty library committee, academic senate, and administration.

And remember, if you don't succeed one year, learn from your experience, and try harder next year.

In conclusion, I hope that you will all take something substantive back to your institutions. And I wish you all an enjoyable few days of good fellowship with your colleagues from Eastern Michigan University and the many other institutions represented here.

FACULTY INVOLVEMENT IN THE UNIVERSITY OF COLORADO PROGRAM

Susan E. Edwards

Economics Bibliographer
University of Colorado

For the past two years, one of our programs at the University of Colorado has been devoted mainly to library instruction for undergraduates. This program is a result of a five-year grant from the Council on Library Resources and the National Endowment for the Humanities. It is based on the assumption that the faculty has the primary responsibility, not only for the structuring of courses and the teaching of subject matter, but also, to a great extent, for determining the level and quality of library use. While librarians may have a limited effect on individual students' use of the library through the reference interview, workshops, credit courses and special programs such as term paper clinics, large numbers of students are not going to be reached as long as instructional methods emphasize only text and reserve books and as long as instructors expect and accept less than high quality library research by their students.

What we are attempting to do at the University of Colorado is to find, with the help of the subject department faculty, alternatives to the lecture-textbook system and to find ways of encouraging high quality library research - within the context of the subject matter courses. More specifically, our aims are to find new and better ways of integrating library instruction into the curriculum and to increase the number of students who will be exposed to systematic library instruction.

In order to accomplish this, it is important to have a close working relationship between the subject department faculty and the library faculty. We are attempting to develop this relationship by placing two librarians in subject departments on a half-time basis. Ben La Bue is in the History Department twenty hours per week and I spend approximately the same amount of time in the Economics Department. We function as liasons between the faculty and the library, especially as it relates to teaching library resources to undergraduates. Active faculty participation is vital to the success of the program. Indeed, it is the core around which the grant has been structured.

The goals of the program were designed by librarians with little formal input from other faculty. Because of this, John Lubans, the project director, Ben, and I decided it was important to find out to what extent our stated goals were shared by the faculty. If the majority were in agreement with the general objectives, we could work on the development of specific instructional programs. If there were major differences, some re-evaluation would be necessary. Also we thought it important, if any effective evaluation of the grant were to be undertaken, that we be able to measure changes in attitudes and practices in the two participating departments over the five years. In order to measure change we, of course, need to know from where we are beginning.

Therefore, earlier this spring we sent out a questionnaire on undergraduate library skills and faculty participation in library instruction to all history and economics faculty, and to a ten percent random sample of all other faculty members. The response rate was over 50% for history and economics and 43% for the random sample. However, the random sample consisted of all faculty - research and teaching, including those who teach only graduate courses or no courses. If this factor is taken into account the response rate for those in the random sample who teach undergraduates was also close to 50%. A total of 58 questionnaires was returned. The analysis of the results was done for us by the University's Office of Program Evaluation. I should like to share the results of the survey with you. Though C.U.'s library instruction program has been an aggressive one, there is no reason to believe that these faculty attitudes are unique to the University of Colorado.

The question on the survey which most directly relates to our over-all goal was one which asked the faculty to respond to a quote from a report entitled, *Reform on Campus*, which was prepared by the Carnegie Commission on Higher Education. The quote reads: "The teaching of existing knowledge becomes comparatively less essential to the task of higher education, and the imparting of skills for continuing self-education comparatively more, particularly in independent study and through the library."

The results [Exhibit 1] show that 39.6% of those questioned strongly agree with the statement, 35.8% agree, and 24.5% disagree. None of those surveyed strongly disagreed. Thus 75.4% agreed, at least in principle, that the imparting of skills for life-long learning has a definite place in the cirriculum. The importance of acquiring such skills, which include library research techniques and the use of library resources is, of course, one of the major reasons that most of us consider library instruction essential for the undergraduate. We asked the 24.5% who disagreed to indicate the part or parts of the statement with which they disagree. We thought it possible for an instructor to feel that existing knowledge should continue to hold its place in the curriculum, and also believe that skills for life-long learning should be more important (perhaps by assigning more projects which would utilize the library and its resources). Though the results have to be interpreted carefully because of a low response rate, there is evidence that those questioned disagreed equally with both parts [Exhibit 2]. 66.7% disagreed with the statement that the teaching of skills should become less essential, and 63.6% disagreed with the clause "the imparting of skills for continuing education should become more essential."

Next we asked if in their courses students are now getting the research skills necessary to locate information in their field of interest after they graduate. In other words, to what extent is the Carnegie Commission recommendation being implemented at the present time. The question was divided so that a distinction could be made between lower and upper division students. Less than 10% of the faculty surveyed feels that lower division students are "usually" getting the necessary skills [Exhibit 3]. Though the percentage increases to 23.1% for upper division students, almost the same number indicated that students are rarely taught such skills. Though, as I shall mention several times, it is difficult to define "Occasion--ally," there is an indication that the faculty thinks that the students are not getting the type of instruction, at least of the type and to the extent implied, in the Carnegie Commission's statement.

One of the other sections of the questionnaire was designed to measure the present involvement of the faculty in library instruction. The first question asked "Do you explain to your classes the indexes, bibliographies, handbooks, etc., in the field?" The results show 25.9% usually explain, 55.6% occasionally explain and 18.5% never explain resources [Exhibit 4]. Here again we run into the problem of what "usually" and "occasionally" mean to each respondent; however, it is probably safe to say that approximately 60% to 70% do not, as a normal procedure, explain the reference tools available in their field. There was another question on the survey which asked, in a more indirect way, the same thing. The answers to that question confirm the accuracy of the 60% to 70% range.

The next question in this section asked how reference sources were explained. For lower division students the most usual method, used by slightly over 46% is to devote a portion of a class period to the subject [Exhibit 5]. However, individual consultation is even more popular if we take into account those who answered "usually" and "occasionally." Approximately one half, at least, occasionally devote an entire class period to library instruction, though it is rare for more than one class hour to be devoted to the subject. The responses for upper division students are similar though there is greater tendency to explain the reference tools during individual consultation.

Because 75% of the sample only "occasionally" or "never" explain the reference sources in the field, it is interesting to know how instructors think students learn library techniques. We asked those who never explain resources how they expect students to learn library skills. The results are somewhat skewed because some of those who responded "occasionally" to the previous question also answered this question. It is possible, however, to pick out some trends [Exhibit 6]. Everyone who answered the question expects students to learn by asking a librarian. The next most popular response is "by the students picking it up themselves." This, I think, we would have to assume is a trial and error process. Also, there is a feeling by the majority of faculty that students are getting instruction in other classes or in their high school classes.

I think there are several implications for library instruction in these results. The first is the faculty's expectation that students ask librarians when they need help; most of us would agree that many students do not. Second, the assumption that students are getting library skills from other classes; this questionnaire shows that this is probably not the case. Third, that high schools are adequately teaching library techniques; personal observation seems to indicate that many students are not getting the necessary skills in high school to use a large research library efficiently. Fourth, the emphasis by the faculty on the students' picking it up themselves; this latter assumption may mean that the faculty look on library research techniques as being in a different category than, let's say, lab techniques and procedures, or it may mean that their answers merely reflect the normal state of no library instruction, or the answers may result from the faculty's own experience.

We asked the faculty how they were instructed in the use of library resources in their graduate program [Exhibit 7]. It is interesting to look at the History Department responses separately from the combined Economics Department and random survey tabulations, for there is a statistically significant difference between the History Department and the others. 66.7% of the historians had formal library instruction in their graduate program. Only 29% of the other respondents had similar training. 57.7% of the economics and other faculty members were instructed by informal consultation with a professor; 100% of the history faculty were so instructed. More non-history faculty utilized a librarian for library instruction. All groups, however, emphasize picking it up on their own. There is no statistically valid way for us to relate this question to the previous one on how students are expected to learn library resources, because of the low number of responses on both questions. However, it would be interesting to be able to delve into this in more detail.

The other section of the questionnaire which I want to talk about this morning addressed itself to the questions of who should be responsible for teaching library skills and how interested the faculty is in becoming more actively involved in undergraduate library instruction. To measure the first — who should be responsible for library instruction — we listed six possible options available for systematic library instruction and asked that each person rank the top three in order of their importance [Exhibit 8]. The third option "within each individual class by a librarian in collaboration with the instructor" was considered the best option by 40.7%. It was also rated 1, 2, or 3 by 81.4%. "In a required class taken by all students in the University" was rated number 1 by 18.8%, but it placed fifth in the ranking of total times mentioned, following "within each individual class by the instructor"; "as a non-credit course taught by an instructor"; and "as a credit course taught by an instructor." There was a lower level of support for no formal instruction.

Two options which should have been on the questionnaire were "a credit course in the department taught by a librarian" and "a non-credit course in the department taught by a librarian." This question should be re-run with these options included. It is en—couraging, however, to see the level of support given to the third option "within each class by a librarian." It is even more heartening to know that the favorable responses were not limited to the Eco—nomics and History Departments, where active programs are estab-lished, but came also from members of the random sample group, many of whom have had little or no contact with the library's outreach programs.

However predisposed they might be, few of the faculty have invited a librarian into their classes within the last year. The results show [Exhibit 9] that 23.2% of the total indicated that they had asked a librarian into their classes, and 76.8% indicated they had not. Moreover the 23.2% is heavily weighted by the History and Economic faculty's responses. If we look at the breakdown, you can see that only 13.5% of the random sample, but 44.4% of the history faculty and 40% of the economics faculty had a librarian in their classes.

When the 76% who had not had a librarian in class were asked why they had not, no clear answers resulted [Exhibit 10]. A reason mentioned by just over one-half was "curriculum is too full." This was one of the surprises in the questionnaire for me, because I had been given this reason verbally quite often when trying to set up visiting lectures. I expected it to be mentioned more often. Just

11

over 35% checked that the material is covered in class which, along with some of the findings I discussed previously, gives us a clearer picture of the faculty's involvement in library instruction. Also, although in an earlier question 81% of those surveyed stated that they expected students to pick up library skills on their own, only 27.8% seem to feel that this expectation is a sufficient reason for not providing students with library instruction. Even fewer indicated that the librarians do not have a suitable background. I think this is another of the encouraging findings, for academic librarians are often concerned about the effects of a lack of a second advanced degree.

Looking at the questionnaire casually, it would seem that the great majority feel that referral of students to the Reference Department is adequate. However, I have some doubts that the 75% figure is accurate. Many respondents will have reached this option with only a row of "nos" above them. Such an option may have been a "good way out" so to speak — that is, something logical to which to answer "yes." However, this is only conjecture on my part. This was another of the questions to which there were several "other" responses written in, and they almost all were to the effect that "I did not know such a service was available."

Finally, we wanted to see if the faculty would be interested in finding out more about reference tools and literature searching techniques for undergraduates. The first question on this subject read: "a review of reference sources and literature searching tech-- niques would (1) reacquaint me with reference tools useful to undergraduates, (2) reacquaint me with the literature searching techniques suitable for undergraduates and (3) I am already familiar with all the important library resources for undergraduates" [Exhibit 11]. The results show that the majority feel they could benefit from such a review. And, to the vital question of participation, 69.4% said "yes" and 30% said "no" [Exhibit 12].

While the questionnaire gives us a good idea what the faculty thinks about library instruction, our experiences in the departments have given us insights into what can be expected on a day to day basis. We have found that the majority of the faculty in the two departments are receptive to us and the program although for many it is a passive acceptance of the program rather than active partici- pation in it. This is not meant to imply that we are ignored, far from it!!! This last semester, Ben and I lectured to eighteen classes for a total of almost 1,000 student contact hours. Most probably, a majority of the other instructors referred students to us on an indi- vidual basis. But active participation, and by this I mean the willing- ness to help develop the opportunities and the assignments which systematically teach library skills within the context of the subject courses, is limited to a few instructors.

To give you some of the types of assignments that I am talking about, this last semester Ben worked with one of Chuck Middleton's history classes, in which the students were required to complete three assignments from six options. The assignments were arranged so that each student had to complete at least one and possibly two library assignments. The assignments were: (1) select an unedited historical document, edit it, and place the document in its historical context by elaborating on the events mentioned in the document, (2) compile and annotate a five book bibliography relating to a particular topic, and (3) write a short research paper based on five periodical articles.

In the Economics Department, I have worked with one class in which the assignment was the traditional term paper, but the students were required to submit a preliminary thesis statement and bibliography early in the semester. The students were then asked to set up an appointment with both the instructor and me to discuss their research plans.

The results from these two approaches were mixed, but one fact became very obvious in both cases: the students were not well prepared for the assignments, even though the students were given a library lecture on the major bibliographic tools and research techniques appropriate to the subject, and were handed annotated bibliographies of the works discussed. It seems it is just not possible for the student to learn in one hour the resources available in, let's say, American economic history, when the majority do not know what an abstract is, what the general indexes in the subject are, or why a bibliography can help them with their research. For both of these classes, Ben and I spent many hours in individual consultation with the students, not helping them with their topic per se, but giving them the background which would allow them to use the library at some minimal level. This takes us back to the importance of finding a large enough group of faculty members who are willing to support and encourage a library instruction program for all majors on the basic reference sources. Unfortunately, in neither department is there a required undergraduate course suitable for such an introduction. So, if anything more than the hour lecture is to be initiated, it will have to come from a new course or from more informal methods such as workshops. The latter seems more feasible at this time.

Experience has shown us that workshops will not be well attended unless attendance is required or actively recommended by the faculty. This last semester, Ben planned three history workshops. Publicity was provided by sending a note to the history faculty informing them of the times and locations. In addition, a poster informing students of the times and locations of the workshops was posted along with other general university publicity. Total attendance was three students, and this is the norm for many of the workshops. It is not enough to have an instructor read an announcement on the workshop to the class; the reading must be accompanied by a strong sales pitch by the instructor. Or, better yet, some assignment which requires the student to use the workshop instruction would be a useful accompaniment to the announcement of a workshop.

My comments have so far related to undergraduates; the situation is somewhat more encouraging for graduates. The History Department does have a course, Historiography, which is required of all graduate students. Ben will be doing a two-week unit on literature-searching techniques for that class in the fall. I have gone to several three-hour seminars over the last semester in which it was possible to present the resources in a specific field adequately, but these students have had some familiarity with basic resources. Also, I have been asked by a group of graduate students to present a series of workshops this fall.

The major problem then, is instruction for the undergraduates who will not be going on to graduate school. Hopefully, with what we have found from the questionnaire and from practice, we can develop more interest on the faculty's part. This next year I hope to reactivate a committee which was formed in the Economics Department when the grant was first initiated. Its purpose was to work on many of the problems I have mentioned. However, the difficulties of scheduling meetings and other procedural problems led to inactivity. It is my hope that working more actively with this committee will make the entire faculty more aware of other possibilities. *This* will be of top priority for both Ben and me this fall.

EXHIBIT ONE

STRONGLY AGREE	39.6%
AGREE	35.8%
DISAGREE	24.5%
STRONGLY DISAGREE	0 %

STRONGLY AGREE
AGREE   75.4%

EXHIBIT TWO

The teaching of existing knowledge should become less essential:

DISAGREE	AGREE
66.7%	33.3%

The imparting of skills for continuing self-education . . . should become more essential:

DISAGREE	AGREE
63.6%	36.4%

EXHIBIT THREE

Are students *now* getting the skills . . . necessary?

    A. *Lower Division*

Usually:	9.4%
Occasionally:	53.1%
Never:	37.5%

    B. *Upper Division*

Usually:	23.1%
Occasionally:	57.7%
Never:	19.2%

EXHIBIT FOUR

Do you explain to your classes the indexes, bibliographies, handbooks, etc. available in the field?

Usually:	25.9%
Occasionally:	55.6%
Never:	18.5%

EXHIBIT FIVE

How are reference sources explained?

A. *Lower Division*

		Usually	*Occasionally*	*Never*
1.	Individual consultation	32.4%	52.9%	14.7%
2.	Class period	22.6%	25.8%	51.6%
3.	Portion of class period	46.7%	36.7%	16.7%
4.	Over one class period	7.4%	7.4%	85.2%

B. *Upper Division*

		Usually	*Occasionally*	*Never*
1.	Individual consultation	43.2%	48.6%	8.1%
2.	Class period	19.4%	27.8%	52.8%
3.	Portion of class period	36.4%	45.5%	18.2%
4.	Over one class period	6.1%	12.1%	81.8%

EXHIBIT SIX

How do you expect students to learn to use the library?

		Agree	*Disagree*
1.	Ask a librarian	100%	0%
2.	Other classes	58.8%	41.2%
3.	High school	68.4%	31.6%
4.	Pick it up on own	81.0%	19.0%
5.	Other students	60.0%	40.0%

In your graduate work, how were you instructed in the use of library resources?

		Yes	*No*
1.	Graduate course or part of course		
	(Random-Economics)	29.0%	70.9%
	(History)	66.7%	33.3%
2.	Informal consultation with professor		
	(Random-Economics)	57.7%	42.3%
	(History)	100%	0%
3.	Informal consultation with librarian		
	(Random-Economics)	61.5%	38.5%
	(History)	44.4%	55.6%
4.	Picked up on my own		
	(Random-Economics)	94.2%	5.8%
	(History)	90.0%	10.0%

EXHIBIT EIGHT

Formal instruction in library skills and techniques should be presented:

		Ranked 1	*Ranked 1,2 or 3*
1.	In a required class	18.8%	40.8%
2.	Within each class by instructor	9.4%	59.5%
3.	Within each class by librarian	40.7%	81.4%
4.	Credit course in the dept. - Instructor	12.5%	43.9%
5.	Non-credit course by instructor	9.4%	43.9%
6.	Formal instruction not needed	3.1%	12.5%
7.	Other	6.3%	12.5%

Have you, in the last year, had a librarian into your classes to explain library resources?

	Yes	*No*
TOTAL:	23.2%	76.8%
RANDOM:	13.5%	86.5%
HISTORY:	44.4%	55.6%
ECONOMICS:	40.0%	60.0%

EXHIBIT TEN

If you have not had a librarian into class, why?

	Yes	*No*
1. Students should know or pick up on own	27.8%	72.2%
2. Materials covered in class	35.7%	64.3%
3. Librarians do not have suitable background	15.2%	84.8%
4. Curriculum too full	52.8%	47.2%
5. Refer students to Reference Department	75.0%	25.0%
6. Others	10%	

EXHIBIT ELEVEN

A review of reference sources and literature-searching techniques applicable to undergraduates would:

	Agree	*Disagree*
1. Reacquaint me with reference tools useful to undergrads	75.0%	25.0%
2. Reacquaint me with literature search techniques suitable for undergrads	82.2%	17.8%
3. Am already familiar with all the important library resources for undergrads	35.9%	64.1%

19

If such a review were offered by the library, would you participate?

Yes	No
69.4%	30.6%

EXHIBIT THIRTEEN

Questions As They Appeared on the Survey

1. Do you explain to your classes the indexes, bibliographies, handbooks, etc. available in the field?
   ———Usually ———Occasionally ———Never (Go to question 10)

2. If usually or occasionally, how? (Please answer each)

	Lower Division			Upper Division		
	Usua.	Occas.	Never	Usua.	Occas.	Never
a. During individual consultation	———	———	———	———	———	———
b. By devoting a class period to instruction of this type	———	———	———	———	———	———
c. By devoting a portion of a class period	———	———	———	———	———	———
d. By devoting more than than one class period to this type of instruction	———	———	———	———	———	———
e. Other———————	———	———	———	———	———	———

3. If you DO NOT explain resources in the field, how do you expect students to learn to use the library? (If you answered
   question 9a, skip this one)

	Agree	Disagree
a. By asking a librarian	———	—————
b. By learning it in other classes	———	—————
c. By learning it in high school	———	—————

d. By picking it up by themselves   ----   -----
e. From other students   ----   -----
f. Other ———————————   ----   -----

Please respond to this statement in items 4 and 5. Thank you.

In *Reform on Campus*, the Carnegie Commission on Higher Education has stated: "The teaching of existing knowledge becomes comparatively less essential to the task of higher education, and the imparting of skills for continuing self-education comparatively more, particularly in independent study and through the library."

4. Referring to the above statement, do you: (Check one)

         ————————strongly agree
         ————————agree
         ————————disagree
         ————————strongly disagree (Go to question 4a)

4a. With which part of the statement do you disagree?

	Yes	No
a. The teaching of existing knowledge should become less essential	--	--
b. The imparting of skills for continuing self-education through use of libraries and independent study should become more essential	--	--

5. In their courses students are *now* getting the research skills necessary to locate information in their field of interest after they graduate: (Please answer all).

Lower Division	*Upper Division*
---Usually	---Usually
---Occasionally	---Occasionally
---Rarely	---Rarely

6. A review of reference sources applicable to undergraduates and literature searching techniques would:

	Agree	Disagree
a. reacquaint me with the reference tools useful to undergraduates	----	----

21

    b. reacquaint me with the literature
       searching techniques suitable
       for undergraduates   —   —
    c. I am already familiar with
       all the important library sources
       for undergraduates   —   —

7. If such a review were offered by the library, would you participate?

                —YES   —NO

8. In YOUR graduate work, were you instructed in the use of library resources through: (Please check all)

	Yes	No
a. a graduate course in or part of a course in library research taught by (———Departmental Faculty, or ———Librarian)	—	—
b. informal consulation with professor	—	—
c. informal consultation with librarian	—	—
d. picked up on my own	—	—

9. Have you, in the last year, had a librarian in to your classes to
   explain library resources and literature searching techniques:

            —YES   —NO (Go to question 10)

10. If not, which of the reasons apply? (Please check all)

	Yes	No
a. students should know the sources or find out independently	—	—
b. material is covered in class	—	—
c. librarians usually do not have a suitable background in my subject area	—	—
d. curriculum is too full	—	—
e. students are referred to library reference department	—	
f. other ——————————————		

LIBRARY INSTRUCTION;
As Seen by My Hairdresser, My Eighth Grade Son, My Freshman English Class at the University of Michigan and Me

Jeanne W. Halpern
Graduate Student Teaching Assistant, English Department
University of Michigan

When I was having my hair cut last week and jotting down notes for this talk, my hairdresser asked me what I was writing. I told him briefly that I was going to say a few things at a panel on library instruction. Before I'd finished my sentence, he said, "Oh, you don't have to tell *me* about *that*! I had it in fourth grade, eighth grade, and eleventh grade, with a week-long review just before I quit college!"

"Well, Tim," I said, "that just goes to show you how lopsided the world is. Last month I went up to the Forsythe Junior High School library with my eighth grade son. He insisted that the library had no books on Paul Revere, and I insisted that he prove this to me in the card catalogue. He proceeded to riffle through the P-drawer, showed me one record entitled, "Paul Revere's Ride," and gloated, "Well, that's it!" he said. "That's their only Paul Revere."

"But you haven't looked under the R's," I said. "That's where Revere would be, just like in the phone book."

"Naw," he insisted, "they must do it by titles here, or else this record wouldn't be under P."

I proceeded to ask the librarian what sort of library instruction this school had, and she assured me that if a child couldn't find something, he had only to ask. "Kids," she suggested, "don't need formal instruction before college."

I could tell these two trivial tales to illustrate what I consider a dilemma of library instruction: the dilemma of too much or too little. It's rather clear to me that Tim could have lived happily with less library training, while a lesson or two clearly would have enhanced my son's book-hunting. I know this is a problem that persists at the college level because it is one that my own freshman students and I, as a graduate student, have faced. And it is further complicated at the college level because it is not just a question of too much or too little, but a question, also, of timing. There are times when what seems to be too much library instruction at one point would be just the right amount at another.

As a graduate student, I took a class in English Language and Linguistics at the University of Michigan. This class spent half its time for the first half of the term with Mary George, Graduate Reference Librarian, in what I then thought was a very exciting introduction to language reference materials in the library. My conclusion now, one and one-half years after the course when I'm writing my dissertation, is that I have to go back to Mary to find what I need — and that's not just because the Graduate Library has been reorganized since I took the course. The real reason, I think, is that I never did put any of the information I received to use; it remains a set of notes in my English 611 notebook. To get acquainted with using reference materials at this level, I should have had the opportunity to take a course like this on my own when I needed it. Or else I should have been put through my paces somehow; I should have had to use all the resources I learned about.

As a result of this sense of dissatisfaction with my preparation, I decided the following year to introduce my own class in freshman composition to the UGLI (as the Undergraduate Library at the University of Michigan is affectionately known) in a more practical way. When the term began, I made arrangements with Sheila Rice, Orientation Librarian at the Undergraduate Library. We planned a three-session unit that would coincide with the major research writing assignment in the course.

This mini-unit in library use began on a Friday morning toward the end of October. During that first hour Sheila introduced the students to the catalogue, filing procedures, and reference materials, with some idea of how these might be used. Each of the students gave her a sheet on which he or she had written a topic and possible subtopics. Next morning, Sheila gave each student a library worksheet which he or she spent between one and two hours filling in. The paper included spaces for subject headings, catalogue work, reference book work, index work, periodical lists, encyclopedia references, etc. Saturday morning was thus the time when they could apply what they had learned the previous day and at the same time get ahead on their final paper — and all this with individual help when necessary. (I must add that my students were unbelievably fortunate since that particular Saturday was part of a football weekend, and the UGLI was clearly all theirs.) Monday, the students had a rather personalized orientation to library services and equipment. By the following week, the students had narrowed down their topics sufficiently to hand in their completed bibliographies. They also prepared evaluations for Sheila Rice which she used in developing further instructional sessions of this type.

Some of the changes she made on the basis of student evaluations now remind me of the problems of my hairdresser and my

24

eighth grade son. First of all, since perhaps a third of the students had had, in high school or elsewhere, introductions to library use, she devised a pre-test to determine which students actually needed the first part of the session. Second, she decided to give the introduction to facilities on the first day along with the pre-test so that all students were adequately oriented to the library layout and procedures. And, she decided to invent small-group library experiences before unleashing each student on his own. Actually, the evaluations were extremely fruitful and interesting; the area of greatest unanimity was that while the experience as a whole was useful, the Saturday morning session was most outstanding because it provided individualized attention to a goal-oriented project.

My own evaluation of this session was that it succeeded in making the students comfortable with the library layout, procedures, materials, and staff. It was, in other words, a successful introduction. My hesitations were those that are closely associated with my feelings about teaching freshmen research writing in general. I am not at all sure that most incoming students will be required to do extensive research at this library during their four years at Michigan. And I am not just thinking of those who go on to become nurses or music majors; I am thinking of those hundreds or thousands of students who use the small, specialized divisional libraries. They, like my hairdresser, could probably have lived happily without the whole lesson Sheila and I devised. As with driving, there is really no reason to take lessons if you never plan to get in the driver's seat. And there is plenty of time to learn when and if, in fact, you decide to drive.

This brings me to the conclusion that the value of library instruction varies with the individual. For some students, it is never really necessary. It is largely the instructor in any given course who decides whether his students will need it. For example, in undergraduate English literature classes, instructors often prefer to have students look closely at the text itself. This is a very hard thing to get some students to do; they would much rather look up what others have written. Therefore, many teachers discourage library use at this level. On the other hand, in a graduate course in a field such as Renaissance poetry or modern criticism, I think most of us would agree that library research is useful and often necessary. In general, it seems to me that except for orientation or individual assistance, library instruction is most effective when related to a course. Credit for library instruction or bibliography might be given when related to research in a specific area of study, as it now is, I believe, in American Culture and for Master's candidates in English at the University of Michigan.

Furthermore, I am not persuaded that a minimum library competence should be a requirement for an undergraduate degree. While it seems like a good idea, I simply cannot see the point of requiring that a prospective physical education teacher or harpist have bibliographic skills, any more than I can see the necessity for me to study chemistry, though it might be fun, I admit. When a particular discipline like psychology or political science or pre-med requires a knowledge of bibliographic skills, that is the time for the student to learn them.

On the graduate level, it is often a different matter. I would strongly recommend offering a course in bibliography taught by librarians in association with area specialists at an appropriate time in the individual's program. By appropriate, I mean a time when the demands of research make it useful to have such skills at your fingertips. Clearly, the success of a course like this requires a great deal of support from the graduate faculty in any department, and I think this is a field that instruction librarians should plow assiduously.

Here are a few ideas that librarians might consider to encourage library instruction at both the undergraduate and graduate levels:

They might offer stimulating orientation tours at the beginning of each term at which students can sign up for a short-term course or for specialized instruction.

They might sell faculty on cooperative endeavors such as the one Sheila Rice and I worked out or the one she concocted with a professor of psychology. As a matter of fact, if I hadn't heard at the first freshman composition meeting that Sheila had done this before, the idea might never have occurred to me. Therefore, it seems to me that librarians would do well to attend early teaching fellow and general departmental meetings and announce that they are willing to do a mini-course with an individual teacher or a group of teachers. It might also be possible to announce your availability for such work in a faculty-student newsletter, such as our *University Record*, and on bulletin boards. Personally, I think many professors would be delighted to make use of such a service.

In keeping with the preceding idea, I would also offer each incoming faculty member — and old timers, too, if they wish — a personal invitation to a group tour of the facilities at your library. I know that many faculty members are relatively unfamiliar with the variety of services offered by libraries. It is necessary, also, to get across the fact that while many pieces of modern equipment may be new, they are not difficult to use.

In general, then, I will conclude as I began. Librarians have a difficult task in choosing the middle ground between offering students too much, which implies more than they need at the moment, and too little, which implies less than they need to do a competent job in their classes. Somehow, librarians must offer orientation and enough instruction to get the students through the programs and courses they choose. For this, I believe, faculty cooperation is a necessity.

A BIOLOGY PROFESSOR
LOOKS AT LIBRARY INSTRUCTION

William H. Harvey
Assistant Professor of Biology
Earlham College

I suspect that I have always been a library-oriented person. As a child I loved books and collections of books; thus, I was no stranger to libraries. However, my first experience with formal library instruction occurred on the second day of my freshman orientation week at college when we were subjected to about six very long and tedious hours of library instruction. Obviously, the material discussed that day made little impression on me because I remember my undergraduate college library not as a repository of knowledge, but as a place where one met people, studied (it was quieter than the dorms), and occasionally had to go to check out a book or two to write a research paper. How one got to the right book or reference was more accidental than planned; for my idea of search strategy at that time had nothing to do with the actual use of a library. To make a critical evaluation of the best resources available had not occurred to me; my concern was simply whether I had dealt adequately with what little material I did find.

My trial by fire came in graduate school when, in preparation for my courses and research, I began a literature survey. It was soon apparent to one of the librarians that I was "spinning my wheels," and she proceeded with patience and concern to show me — over a period of days — that libraries were very systematically arranged places where one could find an important source quickly and efficiently. With the mastery of these new skills, the library became a powerful learning device for me. Now, however, when I look back on those experiences and realize how little I knew, I can see how much easier my job as a graduate student and beginning teacher could have been had I been subjected to a carefully structured form of library instruction as an undergraduate.

I was introduced to the concept of course-related library instruction when I joined the biology faculty at Earlham College three years ago. One of my responsibilities was to coordinate one term of the two-term General Biology course. During the initial planning stages for this course, I was approached by Tom Kirk, our science

29

librarian, who indicated to me some of the previous practices of course-related library instruction used in the biology courses. He asked if I had any ideas about how we might maximize library instruction and usage in the course I was planning for the fall. I suspect Tom knew that I had no experience with course-related library instruction and probably knew that I could offer few viable suggestions. Nevertheless, he took the initiative, approached me in a diplomatic and concerned manner, and before that first meeting was over had not only begun to educate me in library instruction, but made me wonder why I had not thought of all this by myself! I was aware that one of the primary behavioral objectives of the biology department, and the entire college for that matter, is to aid the student in the development of skills with which he can best educate himself. Obviously, one of the most important of these skills is effective library usage.

As far as the Biology Department is concerned, we begin training students in this area in the introductory General Biology program, and by virtue of cooperation between the library faculty and the biology faculty, we have effective ongoing library instruction incorporated into all of our upper level courses as well.

Most of the library instruction in General Biology occurs at four levels:

1. An introduction to the plan of the library in a regular laboratory period. The faculty member is encouraged and usually does participate in this session with the librarian.
2. A guided exercise which is a self-paced search strategy guide prepared by our science librarian.
3. Experience in the library through library "examinations" which are brief research papers of about 1000 words.
4. Use of the library in designing or interpreting laboratory experiments.

There are a number of educational objectives that underlie this concentration in library skills at the introductory and upper class levels. These include:

1. the ability to retrieve information efficiently,
2. the ability to read scientific literature critically,
3. the ability to use scientific literature in problem solving, and
4. the ability to communicate one's biological investigations.

Thus the library, through the use of library-related assignments, becomes heavily integrated into the fabric of all the courses in our department. We are a faculty enthusiastic about the value of the library as a focus in our courses and are committed to the needs of students in library usage.

Enthusiasm is a highly contagious disease and it appears that our enthusiasm has paid off; for our students are not only motivated to use our libraries, which of course is the key to it all, but they do so with enthusiasm and skills that I certainly never acquired at the same educational level. It goes without saying that the faculty member is also learning a great deal in the process. For these reasons, I favor course-related library instruction over a separate library instruction course. I believe that the student is more successfully motivated to use the library when library skills are integrated into the curriculum as a fundamental component of the learning process or philosophy of a course. Skills become real for students when relevant examples presented as a demonstration by the librarian can focus reference sources and devices on a specific library assignment. The students' efforts can then result in a definite expansion of the classroom experience that is faculty reinforced.

It should be apparent from my remarks up to this point that I strongly believe instruction in library usage should be an educational objective of any undergraduate institution worth its salt. Obviously my preferred method for accomplishing this objective would be the integration of library skills as such an integral part of the classroom experience that no student could successfully complete a course of study without mastery of library usage. Library skills are important for all educated persons, but since library skills are especially important for the student who is graduate school bound, one might propose that some questions on library usage be included in a portion of the Graduate Record Exam.

Perhaps one effective way to successfully integrate the library into the curriculum would be in the area of bibliographic instruction for the faculty. Do not assume that faculty members outside their own narrow research interest know how to use a library efficiently. Even though teachers may attempt and perhaps are able to offer their students *some* bibliographic instruction, they could not possibly keep up-to-date on what are available, appropriate and correct reference sources as well as the librarian. I don't tell my dentist how to pull my teeth, and I certainly would not presume to argue with people who are experts in bibliographic skills and reference devices. I don't know how reference sources are really used by students in the library, but the librarian knows a great deal about their use or misuse.

So you see, I value highly effective library instruction. Tom Kirk, the Science Librarian at Earlham College, is a very effective teacher-librarian. He may never know how much I have learned and continue to learn from him through our association and our mutual concerns about education, but anyone who observes my classes or talks with my students can easily see that his initiative, his gentle but persistant persuasion, and willingness to educate this ignorant faculty member in library instruction have encouraged and promoted what I perceive as effective library usage. My enthusiasm for library instruction continues to be reinforced as I work with students who are confident in their ability to use the library extremely well, a skill that is paramount in the process of self-education, a process that will continue long after our students leave our campus.

LIBRARY INSTRUCTION FROM THE PHILOSOPHER'S POINT OF VIEW

Len Clark
Associate Professor of Philosophy
Earlham College

Disciplines are perspectives on the world. Teachers in colleges and universities know that, deep down. We tend to forget it, however, with distressing regularity. We will often answer questions about the nature of our discipline by referring to its subject matter rather than its perspective. When pushed very far, we realize that it's often hard to distinguish between social psychology and sociology by content, however. It's hard to distinguish between physics and chemistry, between biology and physiological psychology, between philosophy and theology. And so, pushed to defend the distinctiveness of our discipline, we remember what we had temporarily forgotten, and reaffirm that disciplines are perspectives on the world.

What do we mean by "perspective"? Although many related answers could be given, we might summarize them by saying that perspective is a way of organizing information. An interesting conclusion follows from this; namely, the way one organizes information is an important clue to the nature of the discipline. It therefore ought to be fundamental, in instructing our students to understand and appreciate our discipline, to see that they understand the way that we organize information within it.

An illustration of this point has occurred in a new course taught at Earlham for the past couple of years called "Contemporary Japan." In that course, a political scientist, an historian, and a philosopher begin by giving students more information, more primary sources than they could handle, all dealing with the Nixon shocks of 1970. Students are then asked to explain what happened in Japan as a result of the Nixon shocks. For the first time students are given more information than they can possibly organize around a given topic. Their confusion is not allowed to persist however, because the historian offers to organize the material for them. Using categories drawn from the discipline of history, he puts the information in contexts and then prepares to draw conclusions from it. The political scientist, objecting to the historian's conceptual framework, proceeds to use his own disciplinary tools to organize the information and to reach conclusions which are in some respects different from that of the historian. The philosopher (of course given the last chance to speak) organizes the material in terms which he sees as especially important. Such a manner of instruction is calculated to teach students something about contemporary Japan, to be sure. But for our purposes here, it is important to note that such a device is calculated to introduce students to those three disciplines as distinctive yet related "ways of knowing," or methods of organizing information.

Why is all this reflection about the nature of disciplines relevant to the topic of library instruction? The relevance should soon be seen when we realize that the library is organized information, and the general organization reflects, in the various fields, the distinctive ways of organization which have come to characterize the disciplines historically. It seems to me to follow that studying the structure of library organization is itself an education in the disciplines, and an irreplacable one at that.

Academic departments in colleges and universities typically see themselves as having two major tasks: the introduction to their discipline, for the general student, usually accomplished in one or two courses; and the development of a major program, for people who are going on to advanced work in the discipline, or wish to have a solid layman's background in it upon receiving the B.A. We all too often see the library as an important resource for research for majors and dismiss its importance in introductory courses. On the thesis that I have presented above, it would appear that course-related library instruction ought to be just as important for introductory courses as for advanced ones, if it is the purpose of those courses to exhibit the way of knowing, the perspective on the world, represented by the discipline to which students are being introduced. Yet library instruction would need to be reoriented on most of our campuses, if it is to fulfill the goal that I have set forth. Instruction in the library would no longer be the teaching of techniques for finding a particular book or gathering resources on a particular problem. It would be geared round the questions: "Why do you look for a resource in philosophy or in history using a given search proceure?"; "Why is the information organized in this way, and what does that tell us about the discipline in which you are engaged?"

Why hasn't library instruction been arranged in this way in the past? Why do not more instructors see it in this way? I think the answer is that we are not trained to look at our disciplines that way very explicitly. As I said before, at the least opportunity, we will forget our education and insist that our discipline is primarily defined by its subject matter. We are trained through a long apprenticeship in Ph.D. programs, and part of that apprenticeship is the cumulative acquaintance with the perspective of the discipline we are engaged in. We learn that perspective so gradually, and so indirectly, that it is hard indeed for us to make it explicit to our students.

Let me suggest the following way of educating faculty to the point of view I am advocating. The next time I tell a librarian: "We need to have X book added to our philosophy collection," what if the librarian says: "Why?"? To that question I might respond: "Well, our collection in Y field needs some beefing up and this title will help." Braving a major fight with a loquacious faculty member, our librarian is persistent. "But why does field Y need beefing up? What does that have to do with our overall collection in philosophy?" I think my answer to that question will typically reveal much of what I think about the nature of philosophy as an enterprise. In responding, I will be suggesting how philosophy as a perspective has led it to consider particular problems within particular conceptual frameworks. I am not suggesting that the librarian deliberately decide to fight with me. At this point he may well say: "I will order the book." That out of the way, and now facing a happy faculty member, suppose he follows up our discussion by saying: "Isn't what you told me likely to be interesting to your students? Why not tell them what you just told me about the importance of this book and the reasons for holding that it is important?"

I suggest that the way in which librarians and faculty members can most naturally be led to interact in discussing library instruction is just where I said it was in this imaginary dialogue. We, instructors and librarians, meet when book ordering time comes. That is the natural time for the discussion to begin. It will fail often, given the limitation of time on both sides, and the impatience of one or the other of us. But it seems to me that repeated attempts to initiate dialogue of this sort will pay off, because very near to the surface of such a discussion lie issues vitally important both to librarians and to instructors as disciplinary representatives. An ongoing dialogue in this respect is something in which I have not engaged, I must confess. Why not? Mostly I suppose it's a matter of time on all of our parts. Yet I promise you that this is a dialogue which both Evan Farber in the library at Earlham and I intend to have concerning a number of courses in the near future, and I would hope that you and the instructors on your campuses will do the same.

ACADEMIC LIBRARIES AND THE EDUCATIONAL PROCESS

Charles R. Middleton
Assistant Professor of History
University of Colorado

It used to be fashionable, in days before modern functionalism in university buildings had made its appearance on American campuses, when constructing academic libraries to embellish the frieze with some phrase appropriate to the role of the library in the educational process. One proclaimed that "Half of knowledge is knowing where to find knowledge;" another, that "He who knows only his own generation remains always a child." Noble thoughts, granted, but how realistically did they reflect the attitudes of the students who passed beneath them? One would suspect that the undergraduates as well as many among the graduate students, if given the chance, would more often than we care to admit have preferred Dante's inscription over the gates of hell: "Abandon all hope ye who enter here." It has always been striking to me, both while a student and as a faculty member, how reluctant many students are to take on the library and to master its resources. Too often the library is seen as a place to be avoided unless one is coerced to use it. It is a building akin to the stadium, a place to go on special occasions and with equal frequency over the course of the academic year, but hardly central to the university experience.

For this image the students are not entirely to blame. Most faculty, trained largely at universities with classy research libraries, look with disdain or at best chagrin on what they perceive as the meagre resources available to them at their local campus library. Why send students there in search of materials which they cannot find? Not only would they be wasting their time, which they could put to better use reading some textbook the professor assigned, but the frustration of failing to locate material must be avoided so that it does not interfere with the process of learning which goes on elsewhere on the campus. The library in this scenario becomes the villain of the educational process. And worse, once the word gets around that the library is to be avoided, the notion becomes part of the campus ethos as if it were written on stone and enshrined in Regent Hall.

These are harsh things to say. They are difficult to live with, and more difficult to overcome. My own philosophy of higher education, however, demands that we make the effort. I believe that a

37

liberal education, a concept which means more than just earning a degree in the liberal arts, involves teaching our students to think critically and to question continuously. We do not ask that our students become professional scholars, though some will assuredly do so. But we do seek to enable them to understand the human condition, past and present, and to be sensitive to the possibilities which present themselves to men with the passage of time. These are large responsibilities, not only to the students but ultimately to the society itself. They require that we view education as a process rather than as an end in itself. In this sense the four years in a baccalaureate curriculum are really only the beginning of a lifetime of inquiry and discovery. It is true that these are the most formal years in that process. Our responsibility is to see that they are rigorous and stimulating. But it is also evident that they are not co-terminous with the educational process itself. We cannot, therefore, ignore our other responsibility which is to stimulate our students to continue seeking knowledge and to provide them with skills to do so effectively in the future.

Many will perhaps take issue with some of these assertions. Today, however, I would ask that you accept them. They are intended as a hypothesis for our discussion here. What they say with respect to our concern about faculty involvement with library instruction is clear. The library, far from being peripheral to the educational enterprise, is central to it. Faculty and academic librarians are partners, not adversaries. They seek a common goal in educating the students, graduate and undergraduate alike. Neither can adquately do his or her job without the active cooperation of the other.

It is easy, of course, to profess these beliefs. But how do we go about implementing them? Most graduate students and faculty, if I may generalize from personal experience, possess sufficient library skills to investigate those topics on which they are working at any point in time. These topics are usually narrowly disciplinary, which accounts for this expertise. Only unanticipated needs, such as the location of a particularly rare book or a piece of unusual biographical information, require that we seek the assistance of a professional librarian for our own work.

Our students, however, have more catholic interests. Even if we had the time, we scarcely have the knowledge or the training to be of much help to them as they depart from the paths we are trodding on our own research. At this juncture, the librarian becomes central to the curriculum. The difficulty lies in how to assure that he or she becomes involved, given our prevailing notions of instruction and learning on college and university campuses. Too active a promotion of our partnership by librarians might readily be counterproductive because it might be viewed as an infringement of faculty responsibility and faculty prerogative. Yet to do nothing merely reinforces the difficulties with which we are all too familiar.

I believe that the place to begin is by enlisting the cooperation of faculty sympathetic to the fundamental purposes of higher education outlined here. There are many among the faculty at every college or university who feel the need to improve the quality of instruction. To a certain extent the development of new courses and new pedagogies enables these people to fulfill this ambition. But these innovations, as with traditional methods, depend ultimately on resources and the utilization of library holdings. Equally important, they suggest that librarians need to be sensitive to these innovations. They ought to make it a point to be particularly helpful to faculty who already have demonstrated a willingness to alter the traditional patterns of instruction. If any faculty are likely to respond to your concerns it is these people.

Throughout we must remember, especially once these partnerships are established, that the focal point remains the students. We need not burden them with required courses in library instruction. I am afraid that these courses too often take the form of busywork or are perceived as doing so, in which case they serve to reinforce those attitudes about the library which are so counterproductive to our purposes. We need not decree that students possess a minimum level of library skills before we grant them their degrees. What we must assure is that they acquire these skills as they seek answers to the questions which they ask or which are asked of them as they take classes, write papers, prepare theses, or study for exams. It is true that separate non-credit activity is a viable dimension of the operation of any college library. Many students surely find the information given in them useful and informative. But most, I suspect, primarily need only portions of this information in specific contexts. Course-related instruction, therefore, seems to be the most beneficial way of introducing students to the library and its resources. This type of arrangement has as well two other benefits. First, it assures that the students receive continuous library instruction which helps them meet specific goals. They are more likely to retain skills they use in specific assignments thatn those they learn in an exclusive library context. Second, the necessary continuous faculty involvement in this type of instruction serves to reinforce that critical cooperation between the faculty and the librarians that we have already discussed.

In conclusion, the partnership of departmental faculty and academic librarians is central to the educational process. Only in regular consultation, in a formal structure if possible, informally where necessary, can we enhance the learning process. The role of the faculty is to set the goals of the curriculum. The librarians alone can assure that students have access to all the resources necessary to attain these goals. Alone, faculty members impart knowledge, stimulate the students to want to know more, and provide them with a few of the tools necessary to assist them in the quest for knowledge. In isolation, librarians can teach library skills, but these skills serve no purpose unless they enable students to meet specific goals. It seems self-evident that cooperation strengthens both our endeavors. Without it students and ultimately the whole educational enterprise suffers.

PROJECT LOEX – THE THIRD YEAR

Carolyn Kirkendall
Project LOEX Director
Center of Educational Resources
Eastern Michigan University

If, as Emerson once said, "progress is the activity of today and the assurance of tomorrow," then Project LOEX could reflect the validity of this maxim. From its inception at the first Library Orientation Conference in 1971, to the spring of 1975, the LOEX clearinghouse activities have indeed expanded.

With the primary objective of collecting, organizing and disseminating information and materials relating to academic library orientation and bibliographic instruction, Project LOEX has been operating on a national level since 1972. In January of 1975, the Council on Library Resources awarded a three-year grant to the clearinghouse to continue and support its activities.

As of May, 1975, 258 academic libraries are members of Project LOEX. Members deposit information via questionnaire and also contribute samples of printed and media materials for permanent deposit and circulation. The LOEX questionnaire has been revised several times, and annual updating of members' statistics is a continuing process. In exchange, members have access to all data in the LOEX files – by letter, by telephone, and by personal contact. Queries about various methods and materials are also handled by referring requests to the institutions which have developed and contributed the materials. In addition, LOEX provides statistical information when requested and continually updates lists of member libraries involved in specific areas of orientation and instruction: for example, institutions utilizing non-print materials in course-related instruction; members offering computer-assisted instruction; lists of commercially-prepared textbooks used in or adapted for credit courses.

Since the Fourth Annual Library Orientation Conference last year, Project LOEX has gained 54 members, received 80 requests for information, circulated over 400 sample items, and will have participated in at least five conferences or meetings in a coordinating or cooperative capacity. A second traveling exhibit is in preparation to meet the demand for this service. The *LOEX News*, a newsletter which includes summaries of LOEX activities, a variety of articles submitted by member libraries and interested individuals, and conference reports and announcements, will now be issued as a quarterly. In addition, Project LOEX will continue to work with the ACRL Bibliographic Instruction Task Force in developing methods of cooperation to more effectively serve the profession and in developing guidelines for cooperation between Project LOEX and the growing number of local, state, and regional clearinghouses on library instruction.

The expansion Project LOEX has experienced since the clearinghouse was established can be credited in great part to the cooperation of its member libraries. The exchange collection has enlarged because members have willingly contributed selected sample materials for deposit. LOEX circulation statistics, in turn, reflect a growing number of requests from enthusiastic librarians interested in discovering additional ways to improve materials and methods. With such cooperation, this national clearinhouse should continue to expand and progress, to the benefit of all member institutions, committees, and individuals dedicated to more effective bibliographic instruction and library orientation.

INDIVIDUALIZED INSTRUCTION AND EVALUATION
OF USERS OF THE CHEMICAL LITERATURE

O. Bertrand Ramsay
Professor, Chemistry Department
Eastern Michigan University

At the onset, I should like to assure the reader that although this paper is concerned with a rather specialized area of library orientation and instruction, I believe some of the approaches to the instruction discussed here will be of interest to a wider audience.

Before discussing the nature of the instruction in the use of the chemical literature at Eastern Michigan University, it is perhaps worthwhile to examine the present status of such instruction in the United States. The last survey was published in 1969 and covered a seven-year period from 1960 to 1967.[1] This was an update of an earlier survey published in 1961.[2] Table 1 summarizes some of the data obtained from these two surveys.

Table 1

Status of Instruction in Chemical Literature

	At Institutions Granting a Ph.D.		At Institutions Granting an M.A. or M.S.	
	No.	Percent	No.	Percent
By Means of a Formal Course	60 (42)	39% (53%)	33 (92)	44% (37%)
a) during the entire period, 1960-1967	47	30%	27	36%
b) dropped during 1960-1967	13	9%	6	8%
Without a Formal Course	97 (37)	61% (47%)	42 (159)	56% (63%)
TOTAL	157 (79)		75 (251)	

The 1967 survey revealed that there had been an 18% to 20% drop in the number of institutions that offered instruction in chemical literature by means of a formal course, with the drop being somewhat more severe in the Ph.D.-granting institutions. The attrition can also be seen when the percentages in the earlier survey are compared to the 1967 survey, although the data are not strictly comparable.

Some of the major reasons given by the respondents for the dropping (or not offering) of the formal course are given in Table 2.

Table 2

Reasons Given for Dropping Course in 1960-1967
(Reasons Given for Not Offering Course)

	At Ph.D. Granting Institutions	*At M.A.-M.S. Granting Institutions*
Prefer to Integrate into Other Courses	54% (46%)	92% (53%)
Considered Less Important than Other Courses	27% (33%)	8% (19%)
Insufficient Personnel	11% (8%)	(15%)

It is clear from the answers in the first two categories that the major reasons courses were dropped or not offered is related to curricular pressures. Whether, in fact, the instruction has really been integrated, or even introduced, into other courses is difficult to determine, and the reader is referred to the 1969 article for more details.[1] Although the survey indicates that the lack of an adequately trained person to teach a course is not the major reason a course is not offered, I would suggest that, in fact, this is misleading since it has been my experience that few chemists are interested in or willing to teach the course because of the difficulties involved.

A few details about the organization of the courses that are taught are shown in Table 3.

Table 3

Some Details About the Formal Course

	At Ph.D. Granting Institutions	*At M.A.-M.S. Granting Institutions*
Required		
Yes	63%	46%

(Table 3 continued)

No	22%	21%
Recommended	12%	33%
Sem. Hour Credit		
1 hour	58%	49%
2 hours	22%	30%
Other	20%	21%
Taught by		
Chemist	86%	97%
Librarian	12%	3%

It is interesting to note the high percentage of the institutions that make the course a requirement. Generally the course is offered for 1-2 hours credit and taught by a chemist. The fact that librarians seem only periphally involved in the courses suggests that the decline in the number of courses may also be related to a lack of communication and involvement between chemists and librarians. How librarians might become more involved is considered at the end of this paper.

At Eastern Michigan University a course in chemical literature (1 hour credit, not required of undergraduates) has been offered for over 10 years. Originally the course used the traditional lecture approach, but since about 1967, the instruction has been provided by means of information presented by slides and tape cassettes. Details about the course have been discussed in an earlier article.[3] Of great convenience recently has been the availability of a compact A/V unit (Singer Caramate) which holds the slides on a carousel on the top and plays either monaural or stereo (one track used for automatic slide advance) tape cassettes. The course presently consists of some 28 units (each of about 10-minutes running time) using some 700 color slides. The problem sets, however, remain the most important part of the course. Each set is correlated with the information presented in particular instructional units.

Recently, I have attempted to improve the effectiveness and organization of the course in three ways:

1. In the method used to assign the problem sets.
2. In the method used to evaluate the students.
3. In the development of additioanl instructional materials.

1. *The Problem Sets*

In the past, the problem sets were run off from ditto or mimeo masters. Each problem contained blanks which were filled in with an individual assignment by either the instructor or student. While this procedure poses no particular problems for a small class, it seemed that this chore might be done more efficiently by a computer. We therefore, written a computer program that produces the problem sets. Examples of questions in two different problem sets (the Form Number) are illustrated below in Figure 1. The italized words indicate those items that are randomly generated by the computer program.

Figure 1
Example of Questions with Two Different Problem Sets

FORM NUMBER: 9
PROBLEM SET 8
(ANALYTICAL CHEM-
ISTRY)

FORM NUMBER: 1
PROBLEM SET 8 (ANALYTICAL
CHEMISTRY)

1) The compound *formic acid* should be pure to the extent of at least —% in order to be considered *reagent grade*. There should be no more than —% of *acetic acid* present. Source in which you located this information:

1) The compound *benzoic acid* should be pure to the extent of at least —% in order to be considered *reagent grade*. There should be no more than —% of *sulphur* compounds present. Source in which you located this information:

2) In the reference indicated to be found a qualitative test for *selenium* in organic compounds. Summarize the test briefly indicating the reactions involved

2) In the reference indicated is to be found a qualitative test for *lead* in organic sompounds. Summarize the test briefly indicating the reactions involved

Source in which you located this information:

Source in which you located this information:

3) In the reference indicated is to be found a procedure that could be used in the quantitative determination of:
Vandium in ores

3) In the reference indicated is to be found a procedure that could be used in the quantitative determination of:
Phosphates in water

Source in which you located this information:

Source in which you located this information:

4) In the reference indicated is contained a general and

4) In the reference indicated is contained a general and compre-

(Figure 1 continued)

comprehensive discussion of the analytical chemistry of:	hensive discussion of the analytical chemistry of:
Cerium	Titanium
The gravimetric determination is discussed on page:	The titrimetric determination is discussed on page:
Source in which you located this information:	Source in which you located this information:

The computer randomly made the assignments from a data base (see later example; Figure 2 and 3) which can be modified or expanded as needed. I suspect most librarians have little inclination to learn enough about computer programming to write such programs themselves. I suggest, however, rather than let this prevent you from investigating this approach, that you contact a member of your faculty who is knowledgeable especially as regards the educational uses of computers. Aside from the convenience in the generation of the problem sets, the availability of the problem sets on a computer print-out sheet has a certain appeal to the students (i.e., the problems seem more important!).

While it is hoped that the students will be able to locate the specific information requested in the problem sets, the purpose of the exercises is to give the students some familiarity with the source materials. The sources to be examined and the kind of information to be retrieved have in the past been recorded on file cards. It seemed that the computer might take care of this chore also, and recent efforts have been directed toward the storage of this information by computer. In Figure 2 is shown the complete computer print-out of two different examples of a question in one of the problem sets concerned with *Science Citation Index*. The right hand side of the computer sheet is cut off from the left, and can be used later to check against the completed question. (Again the individual assignments are in *italics*.)

For those of you who are interested, Figure 3 is a print-out of the program which generates the questions shown in Figure 2. (Part of the answers are not shown in Figure 3.)

Figure 2

QUESTION NUMBER 2	1	QUESTION NUMBER 2
In 1966, J.D. Roberts	1	
published an article in the	1	
journal *J. Chemical Education*	1	

47

(A) The title (and journal 1
reference) of this article was: 1

(B) Indicate (authors, title, 1
journal reference) those ar- 1
ticles that appeared in the 1
next year that cited the 1
article above. 1

Consult: *Science Citation In-dex* (only 1966-67 issues ex-amined for citing authors)
(A) *J. Chem. Ed.*, Vol. 43, 116 (1966)
(B) Hobey, W.D., *J. Chem. Ed.*, 43, 607 (1966)
None in 1967 *SCI*

QUESTION NUMBER 2

In 1965, F. Sondheimer 1
published an article in the 1
journal *Chemistry in Britain* 1
(A) The title (and journal 1
reference) of this article was: 1

(B) Indicate (authors, title, 1
journal reference) those ar- 1
ticles that appeared in the 1
next year that cited the article 1
above. 1

QUESTION NUMBER 2

Consult: *Science Citation In-dex* (only 1966-67 issues exam-ined for citing authors)
(A) *Chem. Britain*, Vol. 1, 454 (1965)
(B) Daniel, N., *Tetrahedron*, 22, 3189 (1966)
Macmillan, J., *Ann Rp. Chem.*, 62, 320 (1965)
Pettit, G.R., *Chem. Ind. L.*, 553 (1966)
Danieli, I.N., *Tetrahedron*, 23, 715 (1967)
Kastrui, T.R., *Chem. Comm.*, 644 (1967)
Knight, J.C., *Chem. Comm.*, 455 (1967)

Sucrow, W., *Chem. Ber.*, 100,
259 (1967)

Figure 3

0, 0, 3, 7, 7, 7, 7
  5 in
  35 published an article in the journal
  360 (A) the title (and journal reference) of this article was:

(B) Indicate (authors, title, journal reference) those articles that
appeared in the next year that cited the article above.
  551965, B. Commoner
  551965, L. Pauling
  551966, J.D. Roberts
  551965, F. Sondheimer
  551966, H.C. Brown
  551965, L. Onsager
  551965, R. Breslow
  25 *American Scientist*
  25 *Science*
  25 *J. Chemical Education*
  25 *Chemistry in Britain*
  25 *Chemistry in Britain*
  25 *Z. Physik. Chem, Leipsi.*
  25 *Tetrahedron Letters*
  60
  60
  60
  60
  60
  60
  60
    6 Consult: *Science Citation Index* (only 1966-67 issues
        examined for citing authors)
(A) *Am. Sci,* Vo. 53, 174 (1965)
(B) Cole, L.C., *Bioscience*, 16, 243 (1966)
    Leake, C.D., *Ann R. Pharm.*, 6, 431 (1966)
    None in 1967 *SCI*
    9consult: *Science Citation Index* (only 1966-67 issues examined
        for citing authors)
(A) *Science*, Vol. 150, 297 (1965)
(B) Calloway, N.O., *J. Am. Ger. So.*, 14, 907 (1966)
    Stevens, P.S., *P.N.A,S.-US*, 56, 789 (1966)
    Strnad, J., *Science*, 154, 260, (1966)

Bent, H.A., *J. Chem. Ed.*, 512 (1967)

Gamba, A., *Phys. Tett. A.*, 24, 64 (1967)

Pauling, L., *Rev. Rd. Phys.*, 11, 825 (1966)

5consult: *Science Citation Index* (only 1966-67 issues examined for citing authors)

(A) *J. Chem. Ed.*, Vol. 43, 116 (1966)

(B) Hobey, W.D., *J. Chem. Ed.*, 43, 607 (1966)

None in 1967 *SCI*

10consult: *Science Citation Index* (only 1966-67 issues examined for citing authors)

(A) *Chem. Britain*, Vol. 1, 454 (1965)

(B) Daniel, N., *Tetrahedron,* 22, 3189 (1966)

Macmillan, J., *Ann. RP. Chem.*, 62, 320 (1965)

Pettit, G.R., *Chem. Ind. L.*, 553 (1966)

Danieli, I.N., *Tetrahedron*, 23, 715 (1967)

Kastrui, T.R., *Chem. Comm.*, 644 (1967)

Knight, J.C., *Chem. Comm.*, 445 (1967)

Sucrow, W., *Chem. Ber.*, 100 259 (1967)

2. Evaluations

The major component of the course remains the problem sets — the completion of at least 90% of which is required to receive a grade of A. It was clear, shortly after the course had been taught for a few semesters, that many students did not exhibit a practical familiarity with the literature sources even though they had completed the problem sets. As a way of checking on this more quantitatively, in about 1970 I included a 2-hour, in-library final exam as part of the course. The exam involved a timed exercise consisting of about 10 questions. The student was evaluated on the basis of both the accuracy of the information retrieved and the length of time required to complete the assignment. The questions are relatively straightforward and should pose no particular problem for the student who has completed the problem sets and understood the purpose behind them. Four examples of the questions are given below (the particular assignments are italicized):

a) Provide a reference to the location of an abstract and the title of a Ph.D. dissertation in chemistry written by *Charles M. Burns* in the period from *1966* to *1967*. What is the name of the research supervisor of the student who wrote the dissertation?

b) An abstract appeared in the *1956* issues of Chemical Abstracts concerning a derivative of a particular compound. Locate the name of the compound and the CA reference.

c) Provide the Beilstein reference in the main work and all of the supplements to the compound shown. What is the melting point or boiling point of the compound?

d) Locate and return the following books or journals to the instructor: 1) a volume from *Progress in Physical Organic Chemistry*, 2) a volume from the *Transactions of the Faraday Society*.

The evaluation of the students by this means revealed a reasonable qualitative correlation between the exam results and the number of problem sets completed. Unfortunately, the test is not so well designed that I can provide you with any useful statistical data. I would be interested in corresponding with any individual who has employed a similar kind of test.

In spite of the qualitative nature of this test, I did feel sufficiently confident of the evaluation to recommend to the Department of Chemistry that one of the master's degree requirements should be the student's possessing a proficiency in the use of the chemical literature. This recommendation was made when the department was considering dropping the language requirement: a requirement that was originally introduced in universities because a reading of German or French was considered essential for the chemist to keep

51

up with the literature in foreign journals. It would seem to me that a chemical literature proficiency is a more appropriate substitution for the language requirement than the taking of a computer course. A student may satisfy the chemical literature proficiency requirement by either 1) enrolling in the chemical literature course, or 2) taking the in-library examination. Most students elect the former.

3. *Preparation of New Instructional Materials*

The performance of students in the in-library examination revealed in some instances [for example, on questions (b) and (c)] that some were not getting an adequate background as a result of listening to the A/V materials and working the problem sets. It therefore seemed that additional instructional materials would be needed. I have found that a workbook designed to be used in the library is the most effective learning aid. The workbook written for use with *Chemical Abstracts* is semi-programmed in nature and consists of three sections. An example of one question is given below:

Question 1: M.B. Kaganskaya is a co-author of a paper for which an abstract appeared in 1961. Provide the following information about the paper:
1. authors
2. C.A. reference
3. title of paper
4. journal name
5. volume
6. page
7. year

Answer to Question: On page 1799, look down the column to the column marked "c." The following information is provided in the abstract:
1. E. Ya. Pashba, T.A. Golkina, I. Ya. Zakharova, M.B. Koganskaya, 2. C.A. *55*, 1799c, 3. "Biochemical Changes Observed During Alterations of Some Bacteria of the Digestive Tract", 4. the "Ibid 102–9" reference to the title is given on page 1789f: *Trudy. Inst. Mikrobiol., Akad. Nauk. S.S.S. R.,* 5. no volume number given (the "no. 6" refers to the issue number), 6. pages 102–9, 7. 1959.

Hints to Locating the Answer to Question 1:
1-1. Consult the Author Index volume (A to M) to volume *55* (1961) of *Chemical Abstracts*.
1-2. In the Author Index under:
"Kaganskaya, M.B." on page 785A is found: "See Pashba, E. Ya."

1-3. Look in the Author Index (N-Z) to volume 55 (1961) under:

"Pashba, E. Ya.

—————, Galkina, T.A.,

Zakharova, I. Ya, and Kaganskaya, M.B.

biochem. changes observed during alterations of some bacteria of the digestive tract, 55, 1799c."

1-4. Look in volume 55 of *Chemical Abstracts* on page 1799.

The student takes the workbook to the shelves containing *Chemical Abstracts*. If after working for awhile the student is unable to locate the information provided in the *Answers* section, he turns to the *Hints* section. This section serves as a kind of reference librarian or specialist. By following the series of hints, the student is finally able to locate the information. It may strike some readers that the sample question above has some rather obvious hints; but the fact is, these hints are often needed. It is not an unknown fact that most teachers overestimate the skills their students (and themselves) have to locate information in the library.

The workbook is only one component of a set of materials published by the American Chemical Society (Division of Educational Activities, 1155-16th Street, N.W., Washington, D.C. 20036) which includes tape cassettes, slides (or filmstrips), a copy of the script, and answers to supplementary problems that are included in the workbook. Presently efforts are being made towards the development of a workbook concerned with the use of Beilstein's *Handbuch der Organischen Chemie*. (The American Chemical Society may well publish such an audio course, but no decision has been made to date.)

The Need for Workshops in the Use of Chemical Abstracts and Beilstein

We have seen earlier (Table 3) that librarians are seldom involved in the formal instruction of students in the use of the chemical literature. If we assume that more involvement is desirable, then we must ask why has this not taken place? Perhaps many do not become involved, even informally, because they do not feel adequately trained to deal with such specialized information sources. If they had such training, they would be in a better position to interact with the chemistry faculty to better inform them of user problems in the library and what might be done to solve them. Two reference works that are often consulted (or would be if the students were properly trained) are *Chemical Abstracts* and Beilstein's *Handbuch der Organischen Chemie*. A librarian with little or no background in chemistry (and/or German) would be understandably reluctant to help a student needing to use these reference works, much less be involved in any instruction. I should like to suggest, however, that such a background is not necessary in order for the librarian to appreciate the kinds of questions a chemist might ask as well as to provide some help in the location of the information. A chemical formula or name is, after all, only an indexing term which when recognized as such should pose no problems in its use by a trained librarian.

What is needed, however, is a means by which the nature and use of these reference works can be discussed by a person who is not a chemist. It would seem that a workshop might be the most effective way of doing this, since (as the attendance at this conference attests) most people would rather meet for a definite period of time for a particular purpose, than read the published literature. Once the workshop materials had been sufficiently tested, self-instructional materials might be prepared.

Whether there is in fact a need for such workshops is not known as yet, but I am presently attempting to find out.

Notes

1) Martin, D.F. and Robinson, D.E. "Who is Teaching Chemical Literature These Days?" *Journal of Chemical Literature,* IX (1969), pp. 95–99.

2) "Report of Committee on Status of the Teaching of Chemical Literature," *Journal of Chemical Education*, XXXVIII (1961), p. 273.

3) Ramsay, O.B. "An Audio-Visual Guide to the Chemical Literature," *Journal of Chemical Documentation*, IX (1969), pp. 92-95.

GAINING FACULTY ACCEPTANCE AND
SUPPORT OF LIBRARY INSTRUCTION: A CASE STUDY

Jacquelyn M. Morris
Assistant Librarian
College of Environmental Science and Forestry
SUNY — Syracuse

There is increased popularity in offering formal credit courses in library research. Such credit courses, on most campuses, must be approved, if not by the entire faculty, then at least by a committee of that faculty (customarily the curriculum committee). Getting a course approved is almost impossible if you do not have at least minimal acceptance and support of library instruction by the faculty.

This is the problem which I will address in this paper: Just how *do* you get a course approved by the faculty curriculum committee?

To fill you in, let me tell you something about our school and the environment in which we created the course.

F. Franklin Moon Library is located on the campus of the College of Environmental Science and Forestry, State University of New York at Syracuse. State University of New York (S.U.N.Y.) is a vast network of 72 institutions which enrolled 234,000 full–time and 127,000 part–time students in the academic year 1972–73. There are 13 colleges of arts and sciences, 4 university centers, 38 locally sponsored community colleges, 6 agricultural and technical schools, 5 statutory colleges, and 3 specialized colleges. The College of Environmental Science and Forestry is considered in this specialized category.

Our campus is situated next to Syracuse University, and we have a cooperative relationship with them in that some of the students' basic courses (e.g. history) are purchased from Syracuse University. This unique arrangement and the specialized curriculum had a great bearing on both the content and shape of the course we eventually taught.

The College of Environmental Science and Forestry is made up of five different schools, the Schools of: Biology, Chemistry and Ecology; Landscape Architecture; Environmental and Resource Engineering; Environmental and Resource Management; and, Continuing Education. There are 1,650 FTES with a head count of 2,400. The student faculty ratio is 14.1/1. Bachelors, Masters, and Doctoral programs are offered in a variety of scientific disciplines with 14 different Ph.D. programs.

Moon Library attempts to reflect the specialized nature of the school with a specialized scientific collection. Because of our unique relationship with Syracuse University, we try not to collect material available in their libraries. In fact, our collection is quite small, around 60,000 volumes with about 1,900 serials subscriptions (this includes periodicals and abstracts). There are 7 librarians (with three in public services) and a support staff of 8.

It would be nice to say we began our educational program in the library with planned goals and a long list of specific objectives. It just didn't happen that way. Our first experience with library instruction was course-related library instruction. This was done at the request of some very library oriented faculty members in the early part of 1973. We did not advertise or campaign; we were invited. In the beginning then, we were pried out of the library and into the classroom. Once out, we were hooked.

Putting together those first few lectures was an arduous task. We had to decide what the student should know about the literature of a particular field and what were the best ways of presenting it. We began by making a very rewarding literature search on the topic of instruction-in-library-use. Some of these initial readings mentioned formal courses devoted to library instruction. Most of what we read was about large universities like Brigham Young or U.C.L.A. and the enormous impact they were having on the field of instruction with programmed learning and media presentations. The whole idea was intriguing but sounded far too complicated and time-consuming for our small staff.

At a meeting of our local library association, it was mentioned that a small college nearby was teaching a successful course. Hearing of their success, for the first time we thought it possible for a library our size to tackle such a project.

After one well-received library lecture, we mentioned the possibility of such a course to the professor. He was extremely interested in the concept and asked a barrage of questions — many of which we could not answer at that point. He convinced his department (zoology) to help sponsor a course along these lines. Within a few days he had even drawn up a rough outline of both the course content and a course proposal. The course was going to be a sort of literature-of-zoology course, team taught by librarians and zoologists. Frankly, this was further than we ever thought we would get with the idea, but this was the impetus for our course, and with faculty support that great, how could we fail?

Further encouragement came when another professor, in entomology, heard about the course proposal and stopped by to discuss it. He had been teaching a course for years that combined the literature and history of the life sciences. He was quite happy, in fact, relieved, to eliminate the literature half of his course. This would allow him to devote his entire course to the history of science. After congratulating us on our efforts, he left saying he would take immediate steps to change his course description and clear the way for our course. All possible conflicts had been removed. So we thought! Obviously the world in general and our college in particular were ready for a course in library instruction. We threw ourselves into the project with determination and optimism.

While we continued the literature search, we also made a survey of S.U.N.Y. campuses to see what was being done in library instruction. These two steps proved fruitful to a certain extent. Many libraries appeared to have a similar idea; but money, staff time, and lack of administrative encouragement were keeping everyone from attempting formal courses. On the basis of our readings, several decisions were made:

1. We wanted to aim the course at the third-year student. The rationale for this decision was to instruct students at the point in their academic careers where they have a definite need for searching the literature. This student, in a professional and scientific program, is usually pursuing his or her first serious research projects. The literature made constant reference to the fact that the student who "needs-to-know" is ready to listen and learn.

2. We decided to broaden the scope of the course rather than limit ourselves to the literature of the life sciences. Concerned that this might erode some of our support, we questioned the professors who had been encouraging us. They still supported the project. The team teaching which they originally proposed was meant to help us get started, not to control our efforts.

3. Searching the literature turned up little information on the exact type of course we were planning. The courses discussed were usually for the freshman level student or strictly scientific bibliography courses for the advanced student. We needed a course that contained elements normally taught at the freshman level (e.g., how to use the card catalog), and yet it had to be significant for a junior science major.

4. Although most of our students have a strong science background, there is quite a diversity in their information needs.

Some of the students are involved in curricula that do not always have a strong science background, there is quite a diversity in their information needs. Some search "scientific literature"; for example, landscape architecture and resource management students. The course would need to contain more than just strictly scientific sources.

With these objectives in mind, we began serious work on a syllabus and materials for the course. The course that evolved was divided into four sections. In brief they were:
1. Introduction to the course and Moon Library.
2. Mechanics of the library — operation and services, book classification and card catalog.
3. Beginning the library search — strategy techniques, some general and specific reference tools, including bibliographies (what they are and how to use them).
4. Serial literature — including indexes and abstracts.

The materials included such handouts as the explanations of the Library of Congress classification scheme, search strategy, how to find reference books. A pre-test and post-test were devised.

A course proposal was composed and sent to the first meeting of the curriculum committee, fall semester 1973, with a cover letter explaining our intention to teach the course starting spring semester 1974. Several weeks went by while we continued working on various handouts. When a memo from the curriculum committee finally arrived, it was *very* interesting. It suggested we define the relationship this new course would have to other courses being offered at the College. We had made a basic assumption: if the student learned how to use the library, it would have a positive effect on the rest of his or her academic life. Maybe we are too far into libraries to realize that there are people who do not see this positive relationship. Because no Library Science program existed on our campus, there was some question as to whether the course could be listed as (a) an English course, or (b) cross-listed in all schools. We felt this course was more of a science course than an English course; and if it were cross-listed, it could easily get lost in the college catalog. They recommended we explore the possibility of offering the course as a non-credit short course in the School of Continuing Education. The committee felt this would allow a broader spectrum of the College community, such as graduate students and professionals in the area, to take advantage of the material. We disagreed in part with this third suggestion. While we agreed there were other audiences that must be reached (e.g., graduate students), we were determined to hold out for a credit course. We believed the other audiences could be accommodated in a variety of methods, for example,

60

through periodic informal short courses or the various handouts available in the library.

We did not feel this memo was essentially a negative response, but rather, we found it encouraging. It seemed the curriculum committee was offering some suggestions for possible improvement. We responded to the committee's suggestions, and several weeks went by with no further word from the committee. We grew a little irritated. After all, this course was going to be taught soon, and final decisions and arrangements needed to be made. Finally, we called and were informed that a memo was on the way. When it arrived, we were really taken back by the words. It said:

The curriculum committee voted to *disapprove* the library course proposal for the following reasons:

1. It was felt that the central theme of the course proposal is, "how to use the Library facilities." Although all agreed that this is an important skill that most students should have, it was felt that skills or fundamental techniques-type courses should not be offered for College credit.

2. The present format was viewed as being restrictive to the potential clientele of the course. Again, the committee felt that a less restrictive format would be in the form of short-courses offered, perhaps, three times during an academic year and, preferably, during evening hours.

There were actually people on the faculty opposed to the idea of a formal credit course in library instruction. Until that point, not one word of discouragement had been voiced. I sometimes wonder if we weren't listening or if we were listening selectively. We had followed every step in the procedure describing how to present a new course. We had support from other faculty; we had worked hard. Where had we gone wrong? We decided to find out what had been done at other forestry schools so we could cite a precedent. A questionnaire was developed and sent to all the forestry schools in the United States. If we could show some of the better forestry schools were attempting formal library instruction, it could help our case. Unfortunately, the response was not too encouraging. The answers were similar to our SUNY survey.

Once the shock wore off, frustration and anger set in. It just didn't seem possible that the course had been turned down. The reasons given seemed weak and more like excuses than valid justifications for turning down a course.

We feel several factors probably contributed to the committee's refusal to pass favorably on the course.

1. We are librarians. Even though we have faculty status — granted to SUNY librarians in 1968 — this was probably the first test of that status at E.S.F. None of the librarians had applied for sabbatical and, of course, none were getting faculty salaries. While two had been granted tenure, this was, nevertheless, our first attempt at really exercising that status in the traditional academic manner. The stereotype librarian image we were fighting to change probably contributed also. Librarians teaching a course was a foreign idea to the committee.

2. Not only are we librarians, but we are among the few professional women on campus. (75% of the female faculty at ESF are in the library.) Having a woman teach a course was probably a very foreign idea also.

3. The library is the "heart of the campus" and a "good thing", but nevertheless a service. One doesn't teach a course in the use of a service, much less give credit for it.

4. We suspect there was also some feeling among committee members that "I had to struggle with the library in a hit or miss fashion, the students should too, after all, any fool can use the card catalog."

5. We were told using the library is a skill and college credit is not given for skills courses. We wanted to suggest that perhaps surveying, graphics, statistics and the like are skills courses but held our tongues.

I guess our anger was noticeable because we were invited to the next curriculum committee meeting. This was surprising and an almost unheard of occurrence. Sitting around a large table over the Christmas holiday in late 1973 a discussion was held and differences of opinion expressed. Many of the conclusions we had reached about why the course was turned down were aired. We began to realize that we had not played the game by the right set of rules. The set of rules we were using was a written procedure for all to see. The rules being used by the committee were not written anywhere.

We were, to put it mildly, completely naive in the political maneuvers of the campus community. It had never occurred to us that we should court certain people, or send out copies of the

62

course description and ask for advice. Other than learning how politically naive we were, the actual results of the meeting were:

1. The committee seemed to understand a little more about our intent. We were able to explain that this course was not to be the only vehicle for library instruction.

2. They suggested that we *try* running the course as a non-credit mini-course once.

3. No promises were made about getting the course through the next time around, but we left the meeting with a feeling of hope.

It was too late to teach the course for credit spring semester, but the idea of the mini-course seemed a viable alternative. However, we disagreed among ourselves about the committee's motives and the mini-course prospect. Some people in the library thought the committee was trying to sidetrack us into proving the course could be run without credit:

1. If the mini-course were successful, the committee could say credit status was unnecessary because the students took it anyway.

2. If the mini-course was a failure, the committee could say the material, methods and content were to blame and thus not worthy of credit.

The alternative to not teaching the mini-course was to spend another eight months in preparation. Our enthusiasm for this alternative was negligible. We were ready (or so we thought) and we wanted to get on with it. Regardless of the outcome, we decided to go ahead with the mini-course, calling it a pilot study to gather data for the defense of our credit course at a later date.

If the project failed, it was, after all *only* a mini-course, and we would have to gain something from the experience.

The mini-course was scheduled to start in February, 1974, and run three weeks for seven sessions. During the month preceding this date, we worked hard to make our materials fit into a mini-course. We also began writing objectives for the course and the four units.

Writing the objectives was the single most important decision we made in the entire episode. Three librarians all dedicated to a common cause still differed about what we were going to teach and how we were going to teach it. The process of writing the objectives helped us think in more exact terms and clarify the course content. We all had ideas of what should be taught and had even organized the ideas and materials into some order for presentation. Writing down what behavior we expected the students to display upon completion of the course helped us determine what needed to be taught. In summary, the course objective was to enable the student to make efficient use of time doing library research. Specifically this included:

1. Helping the student learn the mechanics of the library, including the organization, the services available, the card catalog (both the subject side and the author/title side), and classification systems (especially Library of Congress classification).

2. Helping the student learn efficient research methods, including searching, note taking, abstracting, annotating, and bibliographic form.

3. Making the student become aware of and learn how to use the many types of information resources available, including indexes, abstracts, reference books, bibliographies, journals, government documents, symposia, conference proceedings, and technical reports.

As it turned out, giving the course this way was really a smart move. It facilitated our later dealings with the curriculum committee and also gave us a chance to "practice teach." Some ideas and methods that had seemed great in meetings sounded weak and hollow in front of a class. Above all else, one thing was evident by the end of the mini-course: the students loved the course. The student response reinforced our original hypothesis and made teaching the mini-course a worthwhile endeavor.

Gathering every piece of data we could from the evaluation, pre-test, and post-test; we wrote "The Justification" for a credit course.

This "justification" was an attempt not only to answer the curriculum committee's last memo but also to prove the need for such a course at our institution.

JUSTIFICATION FOR THE LIBRARY RESEARCH
METHODS COURSE
F. FRANKLIN MOON LIBRARY
SUNY COLLEGE OF ENVIRONMENTAL SCIENCE
AND FORESTRY

Spring semester 1974, the library faculty offered a mini-course in library research. The course was taught in 7 sessions between February 18 and March 11. There were 6 sections of students divided among 3 librarians. 39 students voluntarily took part in the course: 3 freshmen, 2 sophomores, 13 juniors, 4 seniors, 14 graduate students, plus 3 individuals from other areas (i.e., research assistants, secretaries).

Each session consisted of a brief lecture followed by worksheets done in class. Information sheets and objectives were distributed at each session in addition to worksheets. A pre-test and post-test was administered via the APL On Line Examination System developed by Jak Eskinazi and Daniel Macero of the Syracuse University Chemistry Department. The results of these tests gave the librarians an idea of the students' level of knowledge before the course and how the course raised this level.

An experimental Design No. 1 (Issacs, p. 37, 1971)[1] Pre-test, Treatment, Post-test, $(T_1 \ X \ T_2)$, was used. M = 13 and a t test for Non-Independent Sampler applied:

M	t	df	P
13	3.7059	12	.005

The sample was small and non-randomized with the pre-test and post-test basically the same. While the need for more data is apparent, nevertheless, the data obtained in our pilot study supported our hypothesis. The instruction (treatment) had been effective. We are well aware that the instrument could merely be measuring vocabulary gains and, of course, all the pitfalls of Design No. 1. However, given that this was a pilot study and in some ways a walk through for all of us, we feel that the statistical significance was also educationally significant. The pre-test also served as a diagnostic evaluation.

Such a course has never been offered by the library faculty before and it could be called a successful pilot study. Having offered the course the librarians now have a greater insight into the need for and feasibility of library instruction on this campus.

The fact that 39 students voluntarily took part in a course and many others have asked for a course seems to demonstrate a need.

Of those 39 students in the mini-course this spring, the majority expressed (via the course evaluation) that it should be offered for credit. Many felt they wanted to spend the time to learn the material, but since the library course was non-credit, they often didn't devote proper time to the material. However, the students said that had they registered for the course for credit at the beginning of the semester, they would have budgeted the necessary time. They also felt credit would add an important motivational factor. Many indicated they would have taken the course (indeed would have preferred) had it been offered for credit. Therefore, the library faculty proposes that a one-credit-hour course be offered beginning in the Fall 1974 and each semester thereafter.

Many of the students in this spring's mini-course suggested the course should be offered in a concentrated format at the beginning of the semester "before workloads in other areas become excessive." Also, having a library course at the beginning of each semester would enable the students to make better use of the library for all other courses in the same semester. Another major criticism of the mini-course was there was not enough time to sufficiently cover the necessary material, and the course should be longer. The library faculty therefore has suggested that the library credit course be offered three times a week for the first five weeks of the semester. Future non-credit mini-courses would be limited in terms of what would be covered, while a credit course offered for a longer period of time would cover material in greater depth.

The librarians do not see a credit course as the complete answer to their educational program and responsibility to this campus but rather one of many alternatives. They would still offer mini-courses to those groups that express a desire (for example, a group of graduate students in a particular discipline). They would also like to implement a formal but brief orientation program for freshmen and transfer students. In fact, more than one of the mini-course students expressed this need . . . "too bad I didn't have this 3 years ago when I was a freshman." Some even felt some library orientation should be mandatory. Course-related library instruction (i.e., speaking to individual classes on specific information problems) would continue to be a viable part of the librarians' education objectives for this campus. However, none of the above would allow the in-depth concentrated coverage of material that the librarians feel many students require. A credit course would do that.

Feeling fairly confident now in our material, methods, and objectives, we again approached the curriculum commitee. This time, before the meeting, we sent a complete package of the course materials, including the justification, syllabus, and detailed course description to all members of the committee, deans, directors, department chairmen, vice presidents and the president. A covering letter asked for their advice and approval. We then telephoned the many friends we had cultivated around the campus, especially the many friends we had made on the curriculum committee.

The only real issue raised this time around was, "Is the library a department?" The argument was shortlived and raised only because each course must have a short title (i.e., Bio 402, Chem 786). The argument was resolved when the course was tagged Lib 100.

The curriculum committee approved Lib 100 and sent it to the faculty with recommendations for their approval. While the faculty almost always approves things recommended by committee, we left nothing to chance. We stacked the meeting with allies ready to speak in defense of Lib 100. An air of excitement hung over the meeting (for us at least) as we prepared for battle. The course was proposed and the faculty approved it without one dissenting vote. It was almost an anticlimax.

WHY DID IT PASS?

There are probably several reasons for the success we had experienced. The most obvious is that we learned to play an active role in campus life and politics. The course was strengthened by the written objectives. These clarified our thinking and made a defense (both written and spoken) easier to maintain. By conducting a pilot study and presenting evidence we were speaking a language understood by the faculty. The committee was convinced that this was not to be our only vehicle for library instruction. Our total educational objectives (see appendix) had been broadened to include several other possibilities.

RESULTS

The struggle has been worth the effort. We accomplished the following:

1. The faculty now seems to accept us as colleagues. Getting out of the library to teach and take an active role on campus helped us gain the necessary support. We went out to recruit allies, but we made friends.

2. Our credit course is successful. This statement is based on the following observations:

a) No real measurement or study has been made, but we feel that reference service has picked up considerably. Not only are there more questions but the questions we are getting are more complex. In many cases this can be traced to the fact that the students have checked out the easy-to-find sources on their own.

b) Enrollment has increased from 19 students Fall 1974 to 92 students Spring 1975.

c) Students like the course. We are told this repeatedly and, after analyzing the students' evaluations of the course, we were amazed at just how much they liked the course.

d) Watching our former students in the library, we know just how successful our course really is. The Lib 100 grads are quite often known by their fellow students as the library experts. It is not unusual to see one holding court in front of the card catalog while explaining about the juicy tidbits that can be found in the *L.C. List of Subject Headings.*

In conclusion, I would like to make the following recommendations to those who are seriously thinking about a credit course:

1. Librarians should learn to be politically aware and take an active role in campus affairs. Make noise. Get out from behind the card catalog and justify faculty status. Practically speaking, get a librarian elected to the curriculum committee.

2. All the faculty support in the world won't help a course the students dislike or do not find worthwhile. If you try to give an M.L.S. in a one or two credit course, you won't have many students next semester. We solicited student advice at every step in the development of our course. Constructive criticism was always listened to and considered; the students know this. One of the primary objectives of our whole approach was to base the instruction on the student information needs, rather than the "here-is-what-we-have" approach. This is not always the easiest task and in fact has not always been possible. Remember also that people involved in the project should genuinely like students and enjoy teaching.

3. We should all take the time to support and encourage our state and national library associations' efforts to formulate guidelines for instruction programs. Many libraries, especially the smaller ones, do not have the time or the money to start from scratch. The preliminary guidelines for library instruction objectives published in the *LOEX News* last year were extremely helpful to our endeavors. The ACRL Task Force on Bibliographic Instruction that wrote these guidelines is an example of the type of organization to be supported.

4. Still better lines of communication should be set up among the various persons involved with instruction and those interested in instruction. LOEX as well as the many state clearinghouses can't function without word from the practicing librarian. If you're doing something, let them know. You never know when experiences you have had will be helpful to someone struggling with the same problems.

5. Library schools should recognize the need (as some of them have) to produce teaching librarians. Courses or even curricula should be available for the student who is interested in pursuing a career in library instruction. In fact, even practicing librarians would be interested in such courses.

The problem asked at the beginning of this paper was "Just *how do* you get a course through the faculty curriculum committee?" I haven't given you a set of rules to follow with a guarantee for success. I have tried to share with you the ideas and experiences of one group of librarians in getting a course through the curriculum committee.

Notes

1) Isaac, Stephen, *Handbook in Research and Education.* San Diego: Robert R. Knapp, Pub., 1971, p. 37.

Lib 100

DETAILED COURSE DESCRIPTION

COURSE: Lib. 100
1 Credit
Fall and Spring Semester (first five weeks of semester, 3 sessions per week)

INSTRUCTOR: Public Service Librarians

OBJECTIVE: To provide students with a basic understanding of the library information process so that materials and time may be used efficiently when doing library research.

SCOPE: To help the students make efficient use of time and materials by acquainting them with classification schemes, research strategy, abstracting, bibliography compiling, use of indexes, abstracts, reference materials, government documents, monographs, serial literature and various retrieval systems.

MATERIALS AND METHODS:

The course will be taught by librarians during the first five weeks of each semester, three times per week. There will be two lecture or discussion sessions each week and one lab session.

There will be no textbook as such, though a list of suggested readings will be distributed. Printed information sheets will accompany each class lecture. Worksheets will be assigned after each lecture to be completed in the week's lab session. These worksheets will give the students the opportunity to work with the material presented in the lectures. Each will represent a part in the process of building an annotated bibliography, the final assignment of the course. These information sheets and worksheets together will comprise a basic handbook or text.

RELATION TO OTHER COURSES:

Basic understanding of the library process is important to every academic area. This course will enable students to make efficient use of the library for any of their courses.

Appendix II

F. FRANKLIN MOON LIBRARY

EDUCATIONAL OBJECTIVES

The library instruction program offered by the Public Services Department of Moon Library shall focus on the user: student, faculty, staff and the college community. The thrust of the program is to inculcate in the user skills, techniques, and attitudes which will facilitate user interaction with information systems and to refine the user's information gathering and processing ability.

This program has five approaches:
1. Credit course
2. Course-related library instruction
3. Orientation
4. Continuing-education program
5. Self-instruction environment and mediated instruction.

1. *Credit Course:* The objectives of the library course (Lib. 100) are to provide students with a basic understanding of the information processes and to help the students make efficient use of time and materials by acquainting them with classification schemes, research strategy, abstracting, bibliography compiling, use of indexes and abstracts, reference materials, government documents, monographs, serial literature and various retrieval systems.

2. *Course-Related Library Instruction:* On request of faculty, lectures are given to students in the classroom or the library for the purpose of dealing with specific information problems in a course.

3. *Orientation:* The library faculty participates in the Forestry Orientation Course (For. 032) of incoming freshmen and transfer students to introduce the library and its facilities early in the students' career.

4. *Continuing Education Programs:* Workshops, mini-courses and symposia are designed to meet the needs of various audiences and are offered to the college community.

5. *Self-Instruction and Mediated Instruction:* The library fosters a self-instruction environment using self-study packages (mediated), graphic displays, study guides and library user aids.

REACHING GRADUATE STUDENTS: TECHNIQUES AND ADMINISTRATION*
Opening Remarks
Connie Dunlap
Head of the Graduate Library
University of Michigan

In the past, instruction on the use of the academic library seems to have been directed almost entirely toward undergraduate students, often only to entering freshmen, and limited in scope to the needs of beginning students. With the press of large numbers of undergraduates during the last two decades, few institutions have been able to give more than just passing attention to even upperclassmen much less to graduate students. However, the increasing complexity of research libraries, the tremendous growth of research tools and materials, the emphasis on interdisciplinary approaches to nearly all fields, and the many other dramatic changes which have taken place in higher education in recent years have all served to underscore the need for specialized training for the advanced student who is expected to do research at a highly sophisticated level. Graduate students begin working on an advanced degree, often with a minimum of training and a limited exposure to the library, and it is somehow assumed that by some miraculous transformation they have suddenly become expert in the bibliography of their chosen fields. Graduate students studying for the Ph.D. are preparing for a lifetime of research and it is vital for them to know how to use a research library effectively and efficiently and to be able to apply the techniques of knowledge acquiry to any discipline or to any other research library.

Bibliography courses taught by members of departmental faculties have been around for a good many years, but something essential usually seemed to be lacking because the professors' distaste for teaching such courses was generally surpassed only by the students' displeasure in them. A review of college catalogs reveals that the number of old-fashioned bibliography courses has diminished greatly. Obviously, what has been needed has been something more stimulating and more relevant to the students' needs — something that would both teach them research methodology and give

----

Reaching Graduate Students: Techniques and Administration was the topic discussed by a four-member panel from the University of Michigan. Presented here are the statements made by the panel members without the questions and answers which followed.

them an insight into the intricacies of using a research library. Just as obviously this was something that had to be done in the library and by librarians who could not only provide a systems approach to library research but who could also do it with genuine enthusiasm, instilling in students a real sense of the importance of the library to their research and making them aware that the library is not just a place to get books but also a place to get help.

But how could it be possible to undertake a major new program — major both in terms of the expenditure of staff time and in terms of the impact on graduate training — at a time when, on the one hand, demands for new services were already overwhelming and when, on the other hand, budget cuts were forcing a reduction in existing services. In such cases, a review of programs and a reordering of priorities is called for. But setting priorities is one thing and finding staff to carry them out is sometimes quite another. To wait until adequate staff is available to initiate new programs is to relegate them forever to oblivion and continued reference to lack of money will be taken only as an alibi for non-performance. It is here that administrators must start to earn their moeny. In any work situation, but particularly in one in which staff will be required to make an extra effort, the most important thing any administrator can do is to create an atmosphere in which things can happen and then stimulate and encourage the staff in order to *make* things happen. Staff must be given the time and the freedom to be creative; staff must be given the chance to try something new and, if necessary, even the chance to fail, for a plan may seem perfect on paper but may in practice prove unsatisfactory — and often more is learned from failure than from success. In any event, the threat of failure must not be allowed to stifle creativity.

Following the completion of a major addition to the Graduate Library in 1970, a thorough review of services was undertaken and an attempt was made to predict what kinds of programs would be necessary to meet the rapidly changing needs of students. In addition to upgrading existing services, a multi-part program of new services was introduced of which bibliographic instruction was a major component. Mary George was given the special assignment of developing a pilot program, and after its successful completion, both Anne Beaubien and Sharon Lossing joined her to continue the development and to begin the expansion of the program. In implementing bibliographic instruction at the graduate level, it was hoped that it would be possible to give the graduate student a thorough foundation in the techniques necessary to pursue advanced research without wasting time exploring countless blind allies or wandering aimlessly through the maze of a large library. It was also hoped that more active involvement in the educational process would improve the stature and status of librarians. In both cases, the desired results have been achieved with great success.

REACHING GRADUATE STUDENTS: TECHNIQUES AND ADMINISTRATION

Anne Beaubien
Reference Librarian and Bibliographic Instructor
Graduate Library, University of Michigan

It is not our intention to present a history or how-to of the graduate bibliographic instruction program at Michigan. We wish instead to explain how we as instructors interact with faculty and with the library administration. But before we do so, we should briefly describe the major characteristics of our instruction.

The basic feature of our program is its focus on the specific needs of graduate students in each department and on the resources for the various subareas within each field. Our large graduate student population — some 3600 in the social sciences and humanities — means that we can form classes of students who share the same background and interests. For example, the 283 graduate students currently in the Psychology Department are enrolled in ten different subspecialties. Thus, I am able to direct my teaching to students in Social or Community Psychology in particular. The same is true in most departments, permitting us to offer custom-made instruction.

Our classes range from nine to twenty-four contact hours, depending on the needs of the students, and have been taught both for credit and non-credit. We limit the size of each section to ten people, both to insure informality and so that we can all fit around a work table in the library. At the first session we admit to the students that we do not know all the answers, that we will be frank with them, and that we expect them, in turn, to be frank with one another and with us about what puzzles and confuses them. Humor is essential to retain student interest in library tools and topics that can otherwise be deadly. For example, we have discovered that students learn the principles of the *LC Subject Headings* more easily with a topic like "sexual perversion" than with one like "Shakespeare" (which, by the way, is found on the same page in the 7th edition!).

We provide handouts for each session which include the complete bibliographic citation and call number of all the books to be discussed that day, with a space after each entry for the students to take notes as we lecture. We load a book truck and actually pass all the books around so that everyone can examine their format, special features, color, and size. We find it is helpful to have multiple copies of the same edition of complex tools such as *Social Sciences Citation Index* or *LC Subject Headings*.

In our classes we teach library research strategy and the organization of the literature. We start each unit by presenting the concept

79

of a type of tool, for example, an index, and by stressing what sort of information one would expect to find in it. We move from general tools to more sophisticated ones of the same type. For instance, when I teach ethnology students, I go from the definition of bibliography to the *International Bibliography of Social and Cultural Anthropology* to the *Bibliography of Asian Studies* in the same hour. Each source covered has one or more examples marked pertinent to that particular group's interests. As we teach concepts we also consider the structure of the discipline and the levels of the literature, from the journal article to the monograph to the encyclopedic survey. At the same time, we discuss how the bibliographic structure complements that of the discipline — the existence of special indexes, subject headings, or compendia.

Our aim is to show students how the growth of a discipline generates different kinds of tools and when to expect that a certain kind of tool, say an abstracting service, should exist to control the literature. Once students comprehend the range of tools and the structure of their own field, we encourage them to transfer the same thinking to related disciplines.

We have learned not to worry about insulting the intelligence of students with elementary tools or basic concepts. Assume nothing and you will rarely be contradicted. For example, this week I began instruction for a class of graduate students in Community Psychology and, at the end of the hour, I told them that we would cover indexes and abstracts next week. One of the second-year students asked me straight out, "I know I'll probably find out, but why would I want to know that?"

We devote the final session to a literature search on a topic given to us by the students. When we present a literature search, we emphasize library research strategy, underscoring for the students how tools interrelate and how they can be used together to solve a specific research problem. Presenting a literature search provides an excellent review of all the material covered.

We stress a systems approach to research, teaching the library as a system and encouraging students to utilize the entire collection, not just a small room of "standard" materials. (This, by the way, is a good argument *against* a specialized "cozy" reading room for each discipline.) We introduce students to important human as well as bibliographic resources, to rare book archivists and specialist librarians in technical services, for example.

The goal of our teaching is to provide students with research skills which are transferrable in time, in place, and between disciplines. Bibliographic knowledge is a basic tool for research — much like statistics. Thorough familiarity with library logic and methodology will aid the individual throughout life, whether in academe or in the "real world." Students learn to operate efficiently in the home institution library as well as in any other library in the country. They learn what kinds of materials and services to expect to find in any research library and how to exploit them. Transferability between disciplines means understanding how the structure of one discipline parallels that of another.

Evelution — "Have you been effective when you've finished?" — is today's burning question in bibliographic instruction. When it comes time for evaluation, you will want to refer back to the goals you set at the beginning of the course and try to determine whether or not you have achieved them.

Attitudinal changes are the easiest to measure. We have a twenty-five item questionnaire on which we ask students to evaluate us as teachers, to rate the course content, and to assess what they learned from the course. Invariably, students perceive that they are better library users and have a better understanding of the organization of a library — but this is not objective proof. Therein lies the controversy over such evaluation techniques.

Behavioral changes are much harder to measure. How can you get a true picture of behavioral changes? Are students *really better* library users? Now? Three years from now? You can start to wrestle with this problem by reading the ACRL behavioral objectives drafted by the Task Force on Bibliographic Instruction (*College and Research Libraries News*, June, 1975). Some modification will have to be made before such objective measures can be applied to graduate students.

At Michigan we have tried several other types of objective evaluation. Quizzes on basics, like what is a main entry, are a start. We also have a pre-test and a post-test with one question for each session in the course. (This, incidently, is the same test, although most students do not recognize it.)

For students enrolled in bibliographic instruction courses for credit, we require an annotated bibliography on a topic of their choice accompanied by a research diary. We evaluate the bibliography for currency and scope, for ratio of books to articles to primary sources, and for bibliographic accuracy. The research diary is a log of what steps the student took, and in what order, to compile the bibliography. This helps us to assess their library research method and to determine whether we are having an impact on the way they go about their work in the library. It would be interesting to compare the bibliographies of students who have had bibliographic instruction with those of students who have not. Eventually, we would like to compare and evaluate the bibliographies of the doctoral dissertations of our bibliographic instruction students with others in the same field. At present we are continuing to explore other approaches to evaluation.

In addition to the obvious benefits of bibliographic instruction to the librarian, such as increased expertise in reference and book selection, there are certain benefits which are unique to graduate level bibliographic instruction. Teaching graduate students not only helps them in their own research, but also has a cumulative effect, since they are also teaching fellows who will impart some of this knowledge to their students. More significant scholarship in the individual disciplines will result from the more effective use of the library. The improved research acumen of our graduates affects their ability to work competently in their own and other fields, which can only bring credit to the discipline and to the university.

Finally, bibliographic instruction is a benefit to the faculty. Having librarians teach research methodology and the bibliography of a discipline frees the scholar from having to deal with this material in class. He can instead devote his full attention to research in his own field. As professional librarians, our job is to know how libraries are organized, what reference and research tools exist, and to constantly be aware of new publications in many fields. We are better equipped to present up-to-date library materials and efficient library research methodology than is the scholar who is responsible only for developments in his own specific field. Librarians are not competing with faculty, since they are teaching "library," not the substance of any discipline. We do not pretend to be historians, literature professors, or anthropologists. We are librarians and proud of it. So far, we have had no problems convincing graduate students (and faculty!) that we do have something to offer them.

REACHING GRADUATE STUDENTS: TECHNIQUES AND ADMINISTRATION

Mary George
Coordinator of Bibliographic Instruction
University of Michigan

The ideal situation for graduate level bibliographic instruction would be one where students would already have a solid foundation in the basic tools and research techniques for their field by the time they begin graduate work. Then we could build from there, after a brief review, moving quickly on to specialized bibliographies in that and related fields and to more advanced topics such as citation verification, locating manuscripts, and search strategy involving primary sources.

We have found that faculty, even prolific scholars and capable library users, do not distinguish between the various levels of bibliographic instruction — if indeed they recognize that such instruction needs to be offered at all — nor do they have a sense for how basic principles and procedures can be readily adapted to areas outside their primary interest. A professor teaching high-level seminars and directing dissertations *ought* to be more alarmed at the inadequacies of bibliographic knowledge on the part of students than someone lecturing to three hundred freshmen, but this is not the case: witness the number of dissertations approved every year without any critical attention whatsoever to the currency, accuracy, and completeness of their bibliographies. Consequently, our experience with faculty and the means we use to pursuade them of the need for bibliographic instruction for graduate students are not significantly different from a purely undergraduate situation.

How, then, do faculty fit into graduate level bibliographic instruction at Michigan?

Faculty have often been instrumental in bringing students together to form bibliographic instruction sections, both for credit and on a volunteer non-credit basis, although we will work with an interested group of students no matter how it materializes. Faculty will sometimes "strongly recommend" that everyone in one of their graduate courses come to us for instruction. On other occasions, a professor may be working informally with a small number of students in preparation for a specific preliminary exam and may contact us about bibliographic instruction for those students. We find this sort of class especially rewarding, since all the students share the same focus, goals, and pressures: there is a great deal of peer support and reinforcement on which to draw.

Speaking of reinforcement, faculty who attend bibliographic instruction classes along with students provide the very best example there is of the importance and immediate relevance of our whole undertaking. There is nothing that will recommend a tool or the efficiency of a research tactic more than having a faculty member exclaim, "I wish someoneone had told *me* about that when I was doing my dissertation, it would have saved me months of work!" You should see the note-taking that kind of comment sparks! There is, of course, another side to the matter of faculty attendance at bibliographic instruction classes: librarian panic. When you have just been informed that one or more professors will be coming to your sessions, all you can do is screw up your courage and remind yourself that you are in a complementary, not a competing, profession. And lo and behold, the individuals turn out not to be ogres after all, but just as curious and captivated as the students.

You may, however, occasionally encounter a faculty member who wants to run the show or who repeatedly interrupts your lecture with unusual cases or examples. Tact, patience, humor, and Excedrin may be your only recourse.

The more traditional forms of faculty involvement in bibliographic instruction also exist in the graduate situation. Just as for undergraduates, graduate students profit most from instruction when it is tied to a particular project or assignment. Thus in non-credit bibliographic instruction classes, however interested the students seem to be, it is always good if they have been told that the bibliography of their proseminar thesis, for example, will be scrutinized both for form and for scope. It is a case of the librarian having the carrot and the faculty member the stick. Of course, you can sometimes supply the stick behind the scenes by suggesting to the professor that such an incentive is crucial to learning and by offering to critique the bibliographies yourself.

In shorter bibliographic instruction series requested by a faculty member for an entire graduate class, we try to discover the emphasis of the course and to decide what categories of tools to highlight in the limited time we are given. For example, we were asked to give several hours of instruction to a graduate course on Shakespeare and the film. Quite obviously, we had to find out which plays were being studied, whether the stress was on classic or avant-garde productions, and how much the students were expected to know about the actors and directors involved. The best background is to discuss both the syllabus and the guidelines for the course project with the instructor before sitting down to plan bibliographic lectures.

As different people have mentioned repeatedly at this conference, faculty members provide all-important public relations and publicity contacts with their own colleagues and with the students they teach and counsel. Their comments to chairmen, to library directors, and to university administrators can make or break a bibliographic instruction program. There is no substitute for the for the endorsement of a "converted" and enthusiastic faculty member when it comes to incorporating bibliographic instruction for credit (better yet, as both for credit and required) in the graduate curriculum of a department. And the *more* enlightened voices on the curriculum committee, the better.

We value very highly the evaluation of faculty members, both those who attend our courses and those who notice changes in students' bibliographic competence and attitudes toward library research. Far from fearing faculty criticism, we often wish faculty would be *more* specific about how we could improve our instruction, both in content and in presentation. They, in turn, seem hesitant to do so, as if they are afraid to play orthodontist to a gift horse. (And at this point we are gift horses! You'd be surprised at the number of faculty and students who assume that a percentage of our salaries is being paid by their department. When we tell them that bibliographic instruction is a service our administrators feel we should provide, they are dumbfounded!)

Our methods for identifying and approaching faculty are fairly standard. We pay close attention to what courses are scheduled for the coming term and to what faculty members are teaching them. We contact all new faculty members in our respective departments and offer to acquaint them with the library system. In doing so, we always make a big plug for bibliographic instruction and our willingness to tailor instruction to their needs. Especially when chatting with younger professors, it is good to ask about their own bibliographic training (or lack of it) and their ideas of what kind and extent of instruction is necessary in their field and at what point in the curriculum.

Every department is organized differently and has a different political and power structure. Fifty-one percent of your success (or failure) in approaching a department depends on knowing your way around that organization and structure. The other forty-nine percent rests on how well you present your case to the right people. Presenting a well-reasoned proposal for bibliographic instruction to a chairman on the verge of retirement can be as fatal as enlisting the support of an innovative and charismatic professor who is shunned as a maverick or worse by colleagues.

Competent and friendly secretaries are God's gift to bibliographic instruction. If you can arrange to be on the mailing list for committee minutes, announcements, and other communiques, and if you can manage somehow to tap the departmental grapevine and get invited to departmental parties, you are really in business! Consider yourself a member of the department and you will be treated as one. Such seemingly minor matters as attending departmental colloquia or sitting in on committee meetings really make an impression. Besides, if you are really involved in subject-specific bibliographic instruction, you would naturally want to keep current on departmental goings-on anyway.

The rapport with faculty that results from reference work, book selection, and compiling special bibliographies for the field is important in securing support for bibliographic instruction and for engendering confidence in your own expertise as a teacher of it. All these are ways of establishing contact and credibility on the job, but don't forget that all forms of involvement in the university and civic communities can only enhance the library's image and benefit the bibliographic instruction effort. As in everything else about which one cares, the slogan to adopt is: "BE INFORMED, ARTICULATE, AND ENTHUSIASTIC. FOLLOW THROUGH ON COMMIT—MENTS". And never let yourself be intimidated. For every faculty member who resists the library, there are five strong supporters who need only to be told how they can channel their support.

Fortunately, faculty supporters of bibliographic instruction far outnumber the detractors, so unless the entire department flatly refuses to talk with you, it is just a matter of backing gracefully out of an unfriendly office to be received with open arms, so to speak, by the professor next door. Whenever I meet with resistance from faculty, I am always tempted to point out — though I've never done so yet — that bibliographic instruction is a lot like parenthood: whether or not they care to try it themselves, they ought to realize that the survival and reputation of their race depend on it.

As a footnote, I might mention some other factors which can positively affect your relationship with faculty. Admittedly, these are factors over which you have virtually no control, but if you happen to have grown up in a faculty family, or better yet, if you happen to have been an undergraduate or graduate student in the department you are cultivating, you will have some invaluable information and contacts to draw on from the start — not to mention that you will probably be more comfortable accosting faculty.

The question of faculty status for librarians has an obvious bearing on faculty involvement with bibliographic instruction. At institutions where librarians have full faculty status and are regarded as colleagues in all respects by the teaching faculty, there would presumably be many more natural opportunities for interaction and fewer psychological barriers between the two groups. At Michigan, librarians have academic status with 12-month contracts and all faculty benefits except sabbaticals, although we are entitled to research leaves. All librarians above the entry level have membership in the University Senate. We find we cannot, however, teach a credit course in a department under our own name without having a dual appointment. This results in our having to "impersonate" a faculty member whenever the case arises. Right now we find this circumstance ironic, but we realize that it will need to be resolved in the long run if bibliographic instruction is to become truly legitimate in the curriculum.

Much initial faculty hestiation and skepticism can be effectively overcome by library administrators doing public relations at their level right from the start. The following paper will discuss this and the many other ways library administrators can and do affect a bibliographic instruction program.

REACHING GRADUATE STUDENTS: TECHNIQUES
AND ADMINISTRATION

Sharon Lossing
Reference Librarian and Bibliographic Instructor
Graduate Library, University of Michigan

There are four basic inter-relationships that exist in an active bibliographic instruction program:

1) The relationship of bibliographic instructors with one another and with their colleagues in the library.
2) The relationship between bibliographic instructors and students.
3) The relationship between bibliographic instructors and faculty.
4) The relationship between bibliographic instructors and library administrators.

Each relationship contributes to the overall success of the program and each has its own set of problems. It is the fourth inter-relationship — the one between bibliographic instructors and library administrators — that is usually ignored in discussing bibliographic instruction programs, and yet the existence of an open and dynamic relationship between the two is absolutely vital to the long-range success and stability of such a program. The three of us have tried to analyze our program carefully in order to pinpoint those elements which make bibliographic instruction work for us, and it has been very apparent that the backing of our library administration has been crucial at every stage.

What expectations should exist on the part of instructors toward their administrators? How do instructors and library administrators communicate and interact to produce a successful bibliographic instruction program? Can we identify those characteristics of a library administrator which most effectively foster and promote the growth of a major service program such as bibliographic instruction? It will become clear to you as I talk that the elements which we see as essential in a bibliographic instructor/library administrator relationship are not necessarily unique to a bibliographic instruction program. They are simply sound administrator/employee management practices. However, both administrators and bibliographic instructors need to be especially conscious of them, since bibliographic instruction is still in its experimental, infancy stage, and like all infants, requires special, intensified nurturing if it is to survive.

The most important characteristic we see is that of commitment, which as one might expect, has several facets:

First of all, is there intellectual commitment to the concept of bibliographic instruction? Presumably the bibliographic instructor has the intellectual commitment, but who among the administrators has the intellectual commitment? In a large system, there are many layers of authority, each with a distinct function. If the top administrator is committed, he will provide both the long range planning and the short range resources necessary for the achievement of program goals. But middle management must also be committed, because it is here that the decisions are made which affect the day-to-day routine: 1) scheduling of work responsibilities, such as reference desk time or answering correspondence, 2) assigning clerical staff to do typing or sorting or bibliographic checking, 3) even such things as making available semi-private office space so that the instructor may have conferences with students or faculty. Does the idea of commitment extend down through the ranks to the lower-level staff — your peers? Will they be supportive? resentful?

In a small library system, intellectual commitment might be an even more critical factor. If there are only four or five librarians, one of whom is the top administrator, there must be an agreement by all concerned on the priorities for the system and where bibliographic instruction falls among them.

Second, you must look at the extent of the administrator's commitment. Is he only paying lip service to an "in" idea, or can he translate this idea into reality? Has the administrator clearly thought out the impact that such an undertaking will have on the system in terms of staffing patterns, cost for materials, clerical support and an increasing demand for more services of this type, a demand which will lead to pressures for hiring additional staff? Does the administrator realize that the time-frame required for the development of an extensive bibliographic instruction program will probably be measured in years, not months, and is he willing to invest the library's resources in such an untried, long-range plan?

The third facet of commitment: does the administrator see himself as an active part of a bibliographic instruction program, not just as a supplier of ideas and resources? Is he willing to make the necessary personnel and responsibility shifts within the library to support a bibliographic instruction program? Will participation in such a program become a factor in promotion, so that total staff participation is encouraged? Will new staff be hired with an eye toward strengthening the bibliographic instruction program? Will the administrator become a public relations agent both to the university community and to the library profession at large?

Administrative commitment is revealed in the creative and support climates which it generates.

Bibliographic instruction, by its very nature, demands an exceptionally flexible and receptive creative climate. Stressing as it does the interaction of human and bibliographic resources, it does not fit neatly into the rigid reference/circulation/technical services framework of the traditional library organization. The work of synthesizing the existing elements and relating them to the needs of students, without arousing anxiety and resentment from library staff, requires a degree of imagination, versatility, and diplomacy more often associated with the State Department than with the library world.

Independence in decision-making is the key factor in a truly creative climate. The bibliographic instructors must be allowed to deal spontaneously with faculty, students, and library staff. Instructors should not have to go through lengthy channels of command before they can make every move, nor will they need to if the extent of administrative commitment to bibliographic instruction is understood and accepted in advance by everyone concerned.

Creative climate includes the opportunity to succeed or to fail, to experience the satisfaction of success or assume the responsibility for failure. Creative climate permits the setting of your own goals and work pace, which is neither tied to an inflexible 8 a.m. to 5 p.m. schedule, nor to an office or desk when you need to be out exploring other resources on campus or conferring with faculty.

How do you know if the climate you have is truly creative or not? Creativity is one of those processes that psychologists, sociologists, and educators have been trying to describe for years. Reflecting on our own experience, we would have to say that if you have a creative climate, chances are you won't be conscious of it for a long while, and if you don't, you will be so frustrated at every turn that you will be aware of little else.

Support climate on the other hand is much easier to describe and identify than is creative climate. Support, like good things and bad things, comes in threes: active, moral, and compensatory.

An active support climate is one in which the administrators establish goals and objectives designed to pave the way for new services. It is one in which the administrators anticipate problems and encourage cooperation from all levels of staff in working them out. It is one in which the administrators react immediately and effectively when a situation arises that requires their expertise or intervention.

There are definitely areas in a bibliographic instruction program which can benefit from this type of active support climate. One of the primary ones is that of faculty attitude toward the library. How is the library viewed by faculty? Are the library administrators interested in faculty opinion and at what level? Vice-President? Deans? Department chairmen? Does cooperation exist in other areas of faculty/library relations such as book selection or reserves? An atmosphere of good will and understanding is very important if a bibliographic instruction program is to be successful. If enmity exists, you had better be aware of it and try to understand the history of the conflict before you approach any faculty member.

A basic administrative function is to monitor continually the progress of all ongoing programs in terms of their original goals. However, since there are as yet no standard quantitative measurements for the success of bibliographic instruction, traditional techniques of program evaluation do not apply. Administrators will need to work closely with instructors in order to devise new techniques of program evaluation. Instructors will naturally be most interested in measuring how effective their teaching has been, while administrators will be more concerned with measuring the total cost effectiveness of the program. These viewpoints are not necessarily mutually exclusive, and cooperatively designed evaluation methods will, hopefully, realize both sets of expectations. If a program is not achieving the desired results, it is the role of the administrator to suggest alternatives or to provide new resources that will bring the program back into line.

Bibliographic instructors should be encouraged to attend conferences in order to learn about teaching and evaluation techniques that are being tried elsewhere, to share experiences and enthusiasm with others in this rapidly changing field, and to become involved in the bibliographic instruction movement at the regional and national levels. Administrators can offer positive inducements for conference attendance such as time off, travel funds, and paid registration fees. But an even more important incentive for attending conferences is knowing that you have administrators at home who are willing to listen to you when you get back and help you to implement those ideas which are relevant to your own program.

Administrators should urge their bibliographic instruction staff to publish. Like conference-going, publication indicates the administrator's receptivity to an interchange of ideas. A willingness to publicize the tribulations or success of experimental programs is a concrete demonstration to the staff that an administrator is flexible, values the educational benefits of communication to the rest the profession, and is not afraid to admit failure.

The corollary of active support would logically be passive support, but passive support strikes one as a non-sequitur, so perhaps the term "moral" support is more accurate.

It is important for instructors to feel comfortable enough with their administrators so that they can bounce ideas off of them and expect candid, thoughtful, and perceptive reactions. Although it is equally important for instructors to brainstorm with one another, administrators can provide a unique, long-range perspective and anticipate system-wide implications that your immediate colleagues cannot.

Staff must have the confidence that their administrators will never embarrass them in front of either librarians or outsiders if they make a mistake. Fear of embarrassment will stifle all sense of creativity, and in the uncharted waters of bibliographic instruction, a staff member must not be afraid to sail into the unknown. By becoming actively involved himself, an administrator can overcome any initial hesitation on the part of an instructor. This will give the instructor the assurance that he will not be a scapegoat if something disastrous does happen. And if the worst occurs, then it is the administrator's duty to help you retreat as gracefully as possible, assess the situation, and try to recover whatever can be salvaged.

Administrators furnish moral support by simply being there to listen, to hold your hand and provide a box of Kleenex. Your fellow instructors will be there to help you with the day-to-day struggles, but it is the administrator who will remind you that change takes time, and effort, and patience. He will need to tell you this again and again and again.

Administrators provide a support climate in one more realm — that of compensation. These might involve both future expectations, such as the possibility of promotion or professional leave, and immediate reinforcement, such as merit increases. If bibliographic instruction is a new service in the library, administrators may have to alter the existing reward system to accommodate the unconventional duties and responsibilities inherent in instruction. Teaching does not fit easily into traditional promotional review schemes which evaluate a position on the basis of the number of people supervised, place in the chain of command, or extent of contacts with other units within the library.

For those of you just initiating a bibliographic instruction program, I encourage you to examine your own administration in terms of these characteristics, and, hopefully, you can predict the ultimate success or failure of the program. You may find you should undertake some public relation work *within* your library before you begin any actual teaching.

For those of you who already have a bibliographic instruction program underway, you might consider which of these ideas could be suggested to your administrators when they ask what they can do to promote the program. (If they don't ask you before very long, you will know that you have a bigger problem than you thought!)

For the administrators in the audience, these are ways that we see that you can actively aid and encourage your bibliographic instructors.

REACHING GRADUATE STUDENTS: TECHNIQUES AND ADMINISTRATION
Concluding Remarks
Connie Dunlap
Head of the Graduate Library
University of Michigan

What do library administrators expect in turn from their bibliographic instruction staff? They expect exactly the same things they expect from other staff — only perhaps some of them in greater intensity. Above all, they expect their instructors to be thoroughly prepared and to perform, in whatever they do, to the very best of their abilities. They expect them to be imaginative, creative, and responsive to new ideas; to exhibit leadership; to be assertive in promoting the library; to evaluate their own work critically, objectively, and honestly; to strive continually to improve library services and library relations with the academic community; to recognize that as bibliographic instructors, they carry a very special responsibility to the students they teach; and, to recognize also that they perhaps must make a greater commitment to their job — a commitment for which they will be rewarded many times over.

I can see only good coming from the further expansion of the bibliographic instruction program at the graduate level -- good for librarians and good for the academic community. Bibliographic instruction, well done, is visible proof that academic librarians have something worthwhile to offer and permits a major extension of the library's contribution to the educational process. At some institutions, some researchers, conditioned by attitudes developed when libraries were less responsive organizations, may initially reject the library's efforts to play a more active role in the educational process and some may even feel threatened, but if the library persists in its efforts, a greater level of respect, trust, and acceptance will result.

Successful bibliographic instruction programs at the graduate level cannot help having a profound and lasting impact on research and teaching — the very core of higher education. We at Michigan are deeply committed to bibliographic instruction and proud to be part of such an important movement.

LIBRARY ORIENTATION – WHAT'S THAT?

A.P. Marshall
Dean of Academic Services
Eastern Michigan University

Mention, if you will, "library orientation" to the average professor, and there will appear a quizzical look on his or her face. It is not unlikely that this amazement will be followed by a question to satisfy his or her mind as to what is meant by "library orientation."

The problem rests in the fact that the answer depends largely upon who is answering the question. It almost always grows out of both the training and experience of the person queried. The real answer lies in the philosophy or degree of commitment of the librarian to being an educator. When we say that a librarian is an educator, what do we mean? What does an educator do? How do we define an educator? Is this term to be compared with our usage of "statesman" – a person who has reached the highest respect and admiration in politics? Do we continue to refer to teachers, to deans, to professors, to librarians, while holding the title "educator" in abeyance until it is time to provide a summation of years of work and an evaluation of a lifetime in which there has been significant contributions to the advancement of the profession? Can we think of the educator as one who accrued a broad spectrum of interests in learning, and who has contributed significantly to human advancement by enlarging upon man's ability to deal with universal problems?

My own summation of the professional lives of many persons in the world of library science is often briefly given as "he is an educator." I like to think that I am reserving this title as one of honor, indicating that the individual to whom I am referring has not limited himself or herself to just the professional aspects of librarianship, but has been committed to all the intellectual involvements of the field of education. So when I refer to library orientation, I am first of all thinking of our roles as teachers, as instructors, as persons helping to shape the intellectual growth patterns of numerous students with whom we come in contact. Library orientation, in the simplest terms, is the teaching of students to use the resources of information and learning. In theory, at least, the resultant product is a person who has learned to rely on his general knowledge of such resources so that he may continue learning for the entire span of life, possibly using this information for the further development of mankind. It is an aspect of library science which concentrates upon teaching, emphasizing the integration of facts learned in many ways to the solution of current problems, whether they be practical or intellectual.

If we assume that any person with the necessary fortitude, mental ability, and motivation can finish college, receive a masters degree in library science, can then have the capabilities of being an educator, we are mostly right. There do creep into the picture other measures which either relegate the individual to mediocrity in the profession, or destine him or her to increasingly important roles within the library world. First, there are those who opt, by their own choice, to seek security and become reasonably satisfied in a comfortable situation. I see no wrong in this as long as the decision is made in all honesty. There are all kinds of personal and human needs which may make such a selection an honest goal. Second, some librarians seek distinction and growth from the vantage point of a secure job, though continued personal and professional growth is a part of their objectives. Through an awareness of the entire library field, they bring continuous improvement and a high level of competence to the position they elect to keep. The third group is mobile. Individuals in that group seek to move from one location to another, improving themselves as they move. Their reasons for moving may vary, but each new experience enlarges the parameters of their experience as they take with them all of their previously acquired knowledge and skills. They enjoy a change of scenery every so often and are even attempting to better themselves.

The librarian who chooses to sharpen his or her skills in what we call orientation may safely fit into either group. He may be stationary or mobile. Only one group, the first, is hardly the type to make good orientation librarians. With the rapid changes in student needs and aspirations, and the efforts of colleges and universities to meet new societal demands, it is an inherent and built-in necessity that orientation librarians constantly innovate and change. To fail to recognize the importance of continued growth and development means failure as an orientation librarian.

There are problems always present in orientation which make the work interesting. The greatest, perhaps, is how to effectively teach the largest number of students to use library resources properly. The answer has to be concomitant with the mission of the college and university, the kind of students it attracts, and the extent of commitment of the entire educational community to the needs and aspirations of its students. The greatest achievement of such goals can only happen when there is a respect among administration and teaching faculty for the contributions librarians and library resources make to the educational objectives of the institution.

The administration of any college or university has the responsibility of maintaining an environment which fosters and enhances learning. There is no agency or department on any campus which plays a larger role in this respect than the library. The professor holds class two or three times a week for one hour each time. For the other hours, the student is left on his or her own. Dependent upon the studnet's attitude about the learning process, much of his remaining time should be among the learning resources. The librarian has the responsibility of making this a pleasant experience. Sometimes there is opportunity to provide excitement to learning by helping students discover something previously unknown. To the less serious student, it is often the librarian who teaches him or her to conserve effort by using the right index, or checking the proper catalog entry. The perturbing assignment becomes clearer when assistance is provided by the librarian.

Perhaps the greatest problem facing the library profession as we end the third quarter of this century is that of image. We often recognize this problem as one which directly affects public libraries, but it is just as prevalent on college campuses. A large number of students regard librarians as a little higher than the clerk-typist. This image is also prevalent among faculty members, professionals, and administrators alike. Unfortunately, many librarians seem satisfied with this less than professional image — at least they do little to change it.

Administrators are not always the best library users. They become so involved in routine matters that they have little time left for visiting and using libraries. There are those who take time out on occasion to visit and seek materials for a speech, or to provide specific answers to a problem. But their general usage of library resources is poor in most instances. Librarians have too often accepted this fact, and operate under antiquated philosophies that the "materials are there; let them come and get it."

I propose that the outreach concept be applied to this group particularly. It is not difficult to determine the major interests of this relatively small group. Individualized notes which call attention to new books and periodical articles meeting those interests are much more professional than many of the little tasks or "busy work" with which librarians are too often occupied. In most instances, the free copying of articles for very busy administrators would pay off in the long run. There will often be chapters or speeches included in annuals or conference proceedings which should be called to the attention of such people, helping them to be appreciative of the alertness of their librarians. When budget time comes, this may mean the difference between more or less dollars, both in salaries and in acquisitions.

Faculties are notoriously ignorant of library resources, particularly of items outside of their normal classification. Many of them are only familiar with the simplest of library procedures, but hesitate to seek help because they think this would reveal their ignorance. Others really think they know enough to find all of the materials they need. Actually, few faculty have developed the expertise necessary to ferret out all related materials in a research library. There is one thing that might be said of librarians which rings true. We have created such a system of classifying books that it even baffles us sometimes. I am often amused by catalogers who have difficulty locating materials which they played a part in "secreting" into the collection.

Faculty can also be served in a better manner on many campuses. Of course, that will take a little thought and imagination, but it will not be accomplished by continuing to be occupied with pseudo-professional jobs which keep librarians too busy to look after the really important matters. After all, a faculty member who is served well will be the best ambassador for the advancement of the library profession and the improvement of the librarian's image on campus.

It is not only the freshman student who needs orienting to the library and its resources. Let us not forget the not so adroit faculty, staff, and administrators.

For these activities, however, we must learn professionalism. We need to keep reminding ourselves daily that our public sees an entire profession through the librarians they know. We need to keep promoting ourselves as educators who perform a function on campus at least as important to the program and mission as those who meet classes 9 or 12 hours per week. Orientation librarianship offers a good opportunity to bring a new avenue to the profession which can provide an impetus to the entire staff to do what they are trained to do — provide people with information. It is good to orient students to library usage. But students should be able to seek assistance from any librarian. So the philosophy of complete service must be shared by all of those who are responsible for any phase of library work.

In conclusion, our professional image has suffered from a lack of professionalism. Too much time is spent following in the wake of others who make the waves. In each library there must be a well-understood mission, a working philosophy. A part of the mission must be to provide a professional service worthy of being called that. With such an image, our colleagues will come to recognize our importance and will understand our roles in the educational arena. No longer will there be a need to provide answers to "What does an orientation librarian do?" They will know that it is merely an extension of an important phase of the work of all librarians in rounding out the training of students to enable them to make their marks in the world of learning.

SUMMARY
Evan Farber
Librarian
Earlham College

Attempting to summarize this conference seems terribly presumptuous — after all, you all have been here as long as I and have observed the very same events. Perhaps, then, it would be more appropriate simply to offer some of my thoughts and reactions, but since I'm not one of those fortunate persons who can give a coherent, well organized impromptu talk (I need to spend a long time making notes and organizing — then revising and reorganizing, and stopping only because the paper needs to be mailed off or the talk given) — this is going to be a potpourri of comments, observations, questions, and miscellaneous thoughts, all within an idiosyncratic container.

The first thing that comes to my mind is a comparison of this year's conference with last year's. While there was also great interest and enthusiasm last year, most of it was expressed by librarians who were hoping to begin programs of library instruction, and were looking for advice and encouragement. This year, however, there seemed to be many more people *doing* library instruction, in a large variety of situations and at many different levels. I find this enormously satisfying.

So many things said by Susan and Ben (from the University of Colorado) were similar to our findings and ideas about methods, approaches, results, and problems — despite the many differences between Earlham and Colorado, in size, programs, objectives, etc. — that I'm beginning to think that most librarians involved in library instruction are thinking and working very much along these same lines. Of course, we still have many things to share with one another, but perhaps now we should be making more of an effort to talk to faculty and administrators, not at our own campuses (I assume we're already talking to them), but at professional meetings and in the professional journals. They are the ones, in other words, who need to hear about library instruction — and I think they would be quite receptive if they understood what it could do to enhance their teaching. After all, we are working toward the same objectives, but I know most teaching faculty are not aware of the things we've been doing at many institutions.

Our experience supports Colorado's observation that students do not really understand search strategy, and that in order to understand it, it is necessary for them to go through an exercise. The habit most difficult for students to break is going immediately to the subject portion of the card catalog. This raises a question:

101

perhaps the subject catalog should be moved, be made less immediately accessible, and be placed so that it functions as a part of the reference collection, a logical step in the search process. We've done this at Earlham's Science Library: students encounter first the general sources — encyclopedias, handbooks, etc. — before they come to the subject portion of the card catalog (the author/title portion, however, is close to the library's entrance), and it seems to work well. Admittedly, though, this is for a small and select group of users, almost all of whom have been given heavy doses of library instruction.

I liked the idea of Jeanne Halpern's students (in her English class) evaluating Sheila Rice, who gave the library instruction, in order to give her feedback on her style and content. I would hope, however, that it was not so immediate that they didn't have a chance to use the materials and procedures she presented to them.

How can we improve our techniques of presentation? As Connie Dunlap (University of Michigan) pointed out, bad lectures can not only kill a library instruction program, they can also reduce the impact of the library generally. Faculty members and students may be too kind to say anything negative (or even worse, perhaps they don't expect very much from librarians). Here is where it is helpful to have another staff member, who can be candid, attend occasional lectures. Also effective is videotaping some lectures, and then viewing the tapes with several librarians for comments.

Jeanne Halpern commented that "some students don't need to know about research," and she named those such as her hairdresser. This, I think, is a prevalent but unfortunate attitude. We have not gotten across enough the wider purposes of library instruction, perhaps not even in our own minds. We need to distinguish between the usefulness of library instruction for writing better papers and library instruction to help students understand the structure of information. The former is basic and gives us an opening to the classrooms, where we help the teaching faculty achieve their course objectives more effectively, but we should not lose sight of the latter function. It is much more theoretical, but in the long run perhaps even more important.

One of the speakers mentioned the importance of "an aggressive attitude" by reference librarians. We all know that what was meant did not at all imply being overbearing or discourteous, but rather always being aware of and sensitive to those students and faculty who, for one reason or another — diffidence, ignorance or over-confidence — do not ask for assistance. That awareness, aggressiveness if you will, *is* important, but along with it should go the awareness that educating the student, and not just giving information, is important. In giving reference help, we should try, whenever possible and appropriate, to show why we followed a particular pattern of search, why we selected one reference book rather than another, even — if the student is interested and receptive — generalizing about types of reference works. Some of the best education can be carried on during these one-to-one sessions, and a student who has learned much during one of them not only becomes much more knowledgeable about search strategy and reference work, but also can then convey his knowledge to others. It has been shown time and again that some of the best learning goes on by students teaching students, and if we can teach a few really well, the multiplier effect will be significant.

The Colorado librarians' experience with their Sociology Department (i.e., complete lack of success in instituting library instruction) reminds me of something that should be repeated again and again: don't waste time beating your heads against walls. There are too many receptive departments and individuals waiting to be approached. On the other hand, as Len Clark (Earlham College), pointed out, persistence is important, especially in reminding faculty members year after year that librarians should talk to their classes. After all, library instruction is not their paramount concern, and many are apt to forget about planning for it, even when their experience had been positive. My own stints at the Reference Desk have shown this time and again, and really, whoever is at the Desk ought to be constantly aware that students' questions may indicate the need for library instruction in particular courses. Such an indication, furthermore, is the best evidence for recalcitrant faculty members. If they can be told, "Look, last night six students asked how to find information for their papers," the need for a class presentation should be obvious. But along with conveying the demonstrated need, specific reference works one proposes to show the class should be pointed out. The basic point I am making here is that we should, whenever possible, capitalize on a demonstrated need for instruction,and the Reference Desk is pivotal in this.

Someone asked me, how can Earlham have a library instruction program without special funds? My response is: it is not easy, but it *is* a matter of priorities. I always come back to the point: what good is a collection if it is not being used effectively? In a liberal arts college, at least, departments are rarely called upon to justify their purpose. The library, however, while maybe not asked to justify its existence, will increasingly be called upon (as long as the economic crunch continues, anyway) to justify its expenditures, and it seems to me that the best justification is effective use. Frankly, I know of no way of insuring effective use other than by a program of library instruction.

The comment was made that library schools should emphasize library instruction. To be sure, but how can they be persuaded to do it? There is only a beginning interest by the schools, and I find it discouraging that at this conference there is not one representative from any of the schools.

There is not much question about their lack of interest. We had a class from a library school visit us a few weeks ago. Its particular interest was academic library buildings, but when I attempted to talk about the relationship between a library instruction program and library planning, the faculty member accompanying the group couldn't have been less interested. Another instance: a request the other day from a library school faculty member teaching a course on academic libraries asked for our statistics and a copy of the annual report. I responded that I did not write a report, and if he wanted to see what we were doing he should read my chapter in John Lubans' book, because that's what we were doing that was *really* important.

This lack of interest is really too bad, because we could use the expertise of library schools in helping systematize the theory and techniques of library instruction.

Sharon Lossing (University of Michigan) mentioned that library instruction really cannot fit into the traditional library organization. In the small library, where there is no formal organizational pattern, or, in any case, where the pattern is fairly fluid, this is not a problem. In the large library, however, because of the newness of the responsibilities of library instruction as well as, of course, the many facets of those responsibilities touching traditional areas of the library, it may well be a problem. Assuming that library instruction will become an increasingly important function for almost every academic library, my guess is that the structure of Sangamon State will be widely emulated. At least it should be carefully examined, and I would recommend reading about it in a forth-coming issue of the *Journal of Academic Librarianship.*

Why start a library instruction program? There are the fairly obvious educational, professional, and practical reasons, but we should not be ashamed to admit that part of it *is* status-seeking. I am not being pejorative when I use the term here, because the status we are seeking is the one the teaching faculty has. That is, we wish to be identified as educators, and that is commendable, particularly since that is exactly what we are doing. I see no reason, in other words, to conceal our educational objectives, and if that is status-seeking, so be it.

I was asked by someone yesterday, "What would your ideal library instruction program be?" I really couldn't answer, because an adequate response would take a lot of time and thought. But then,

I am not sure I want to know. I realize that is not good administrative practice, in which one is supposed to establish objectives and then plan how to accomplish them, but I say I am not sure I want to know for two reasons. First, having a perfect program in mind could well become frustrating as one met obstacle after obstacle. Now, I can look back on our progress and feel some sense of accomplishment. I am not so foolish as to think we have achieved more than just a beginning, even though I think it is a good one. Second, until evaluation techniques are improved (improved? . . . established, really), there is not much point in talking about an ideal, because we would never know even if we had achieved it. No, talking about an ideal program is putting the cart before the horse. We might talk about the ideal evaluation, and if we could ever agree on that, developing a program would be much easier.

Perhaps my feeling that I don't want to know what the ideal program might be is a cop-out, but I do feel terribly frustrated by the lack of evaluation techniques.

Someone asked me toward the end of the conference if I had learned anything new. She had heard someone else say that they were "hearing the same things" — last year, here, a few weeks ago at a conference in Wooster, Ohio, etc. My response was to quote Louis R. Wilson, that magnificent figure in Ameican Librarianship, whose class in library administration I took when in library school. Whenever he visited a library, Dr. Wilson told us, he always carried a little notebook because no matter how small the library, he never failed to note something worthwhile. Similarly, whenever I go to a conference, visit another institution's program, or just talk with interested librarians, I always learn something — about a new approach, a new technique, a new idea.

But this conference was not designed primarily for the benefit of those, like myself, who have practiced, thought about, and discussed library instruction for a long time. Rather, it is for the many persons here who perhaps don't have colleagues who are eager or even willing to talk about library instruction. For them, these few days serve as — if not spiritual renewal — certainly professional reinforcement and encouragement, and they have the chance to learn again that they are not alone, that there are other librarians who share their philosophy and objectives, their plans and frustrations, and that there are programs that are well on their way which can offer counsel and inspiration.

LIBRARY ORIENTATION FOR ACADEMIC LIBRARIES
May 15–17, 1975
Eastern Michigan University

PARTICIPANTS

Arndt, John
Head, Reference/Collections
Wilfrid Laurier University
Waterloo, Ontario
Canada N2L 3C5

Baker, Nancy L.
Assistant Reference Librarian
English Bibliography
SUNY - Binghamton
Binghamton, New York 13901

Baldwin, Julia
Assistant Reference Librarian
University of Toledo
Toledo, Ohio 43606

Bazuzi, John
Assistant Reference Librarian
Medical College of Virginia
Virginia Commonwealth
    University
Richmond, Virginia 23298

Beasecker, Robert F.
Reference Librarian
Grand Valley State College
Allendale, Michigan 49401

Bitting, Elaine
Library Instruction Librarian
Main Library
University of Cincinnati
Cincinnati, Ohio 45221

Blair, Lynne M.
Assistant Librarian
Undergraduate Library
University of Illinois
Champaign, Illinois 61820

Bowen, Albertine
Senior Media Specialist
Federal City College
Washington, D.C. 20001

Bowman, Mary
Assistant Reference Librarian
DePaul University
25 East Jackson
Chicago, Illinois 60604

Bradley, Judith I.
Reference Librarian/Assistant
    Director
Mercyhurst College Library
Erie, Pennsylvania 16501

Breault, Keitha
Reference Librarian
Ferris State College
Big Rapids, Michigan 49307

Brooke, Ann
Reference Librarian
Undergraduate Library
University of Texas - Austin
Austin, Texas 78712

Brooke, Lee
Director of Libraries
Chicago College of Osteopathic
    Medicine
5200 Ellis
Chicago, Illinois 60615

Brown, Lucille A.
Reference Librarian
Sojourner Truth Library
SUNY - New Paltz
New Paltz, New York 12525

Brown, Philip
Reference Department Head
South Dakota State University
Brookings, South Dakota 57006

Butler, Elizabeth A.
Assistant Librarian
Public Instructional Services
University of California
San Diego, California 92037

Campbell, Katie
Librarian
Triton College
River Grove, Illinois 60614

Chojenski, Peter
Instructor - Library Science
Purdue University - Calumet
Hammond, Indiana 46323

Ciliberti, Anne
Reference Librarian
Syracuse University Libraries
Syracuse, New York 13210

Clark, Ann H.
Assistant Reference Librarian
Undergraduate Library
SUNY - Buffalo
Buffalo, New York 14214

Clayton, Ronald J.
Coordinator - Liaison Program
Federal City College
Washington, D.C. 20001

Consolantis, Maureen
General Reference Librarian
Drexel University
Philadelphia, Pennsylvania 19104

Conway, Jeanne W.
Associate Librarian - Public Services
Gallaudet College Library
7th & Florida, N.E.
Washington, D.C. 20002

Corby, Katherine
Reference Librarian
Drexel University
Philadelphia, Pennsylvania
15104

Croak, Margaret
Reference Librarian
De Paul University
2323 N. Seminary
Chicago, Illinois 60614

Dawson, Clarice
Acting Undergraduate Librarian
Michigan State University
East Lansing, Michigan 48824

DeMarinis, Ellen S.
Reference Librarian
Library
University of Pennsylvania
Philadelphia, Pennsylvania
19174

Dickerman, Carol
Principal Reference Librarian
Yale University Library
New Haven, Connecticut
06520

Dionne, JoAnn
Public Services Coordinator
SUNY - College of Environment
Science and Forestry
Syracuse, New York 13210

Donaldson, David
Library Director
Midland Lutheran College
Fremont, Nebraska 68025

Doyle, Richard
Reference Librarian
Coe College
Cedar Rapids, Iowa 52402

Druesedow, Elaine
Graduate Student
Kent State University
142 S. Cedar
Oberlin, Ohio 44074

Druesedow, John
Conservatory Library
Oberlin College
Oberlin, Ohio   44074

Dusenbury, Carolyn
Division Head
General Reference Division
University of Utah
Marriott Library
Salt Lake City, Utah 74102

Ebert, Mary Hilda
Reference Librarian
Saint Peter's College
Jersey City, New Jersey 07306

Edwards, Fern
Associate Librarian - User Service
Gallaudet College Library
7th & Florida Avenue, N.E.
Washington, D.C. 20002

Elbers, Joan S.
Librarian/Library Instructor
Montgomery College
Rockville, Maryland 20850

Ellis, Virginia R.
Public Services Librarian
Miami University - Middletown
Middletown, Ohio 45042

Eriksen, Anne
Population Culture Cataloger
Bowling Green State University
Bowling Green, Ohio   43403

Fallon, Ann M.
Head, Reference Department
Mugar Memorial Library
Boston University
Boston, Massachusetts 02215

Feldman, Beverly
Reference Librarian
Penn State University - Ogontz
Abington, Pennsylvania 19001

Fisk, Linda Fuerle
Assistant Reference Librarian
Behrend College
Penn State University
Erie, Pennsylvania 16510

Frick, Bonnie
Reference Librarian
Earlham College
Richmond, Indiana 47374

Fultz, Norma
Technical Materials Librarian/
   Assistant Professor
Ball State University
Muncie, Indiana 47306

Gambill, Donna
Reference Librarian/Instructor
Memphis State University
Memphis, Tennessee 38152

Gornall, Diane
Reference Librarian
University of Michigan - Dearborn
Dearborn, Michigan 48128

Greaves, James E.
Assistant Reference Librarian
Indiana University
Library
Bloomington, Indiana 47401

Greenwood, Larry
Head, Instructional Services
University of Kentucky
Lexington, Kentucky 40506

Griggs, Bettie J.
Coordinator, Library Instruction
Miles College
Birmingham, Alabama 35208

Grossmann, Mary Beth
Dental/Education Librarian
Dental Library
University of Southern
  California
Los Angeles, California 90007

Hampel, Edith Baker
Head, Reference Department
Temple University
Philadelphia, Pennsylvania 19122

Hardesty, Larry
User Services Coordinator
Kearney State College
Kearney, Nebraska 68847

Heidler, Robert S.
Reference Librarian & Chairman
Library
Bowling Green State University
Bowling Green, Ohio 43493

Henderson, Roberta
Reference Librarian
Northern Michigan University
Marquette, Michigan 49855

Hickok, Florence
Head Reference Librarian
Michigan State University
East Lansing, Michigan 48823

Hoffman, Connie
Reference Librarian
Indiana University East
Richmond, Indiana 47374

Hupp, Mary A.
Coordinator - Library Science
  Program
Fairmont College
Fairmont, West Virginia 26554

Hutchinson, Harold
Documents Librarian
Virginia Commonwealth Uni-
  versity
Richmond, Virginia 23284

Jennerich, Elaine
Reference Librarian
Baylor University
Waco, Texas 76706

Johnson, Irma Y.
Science Librarian
Massachusetts Institute of
  Technology
Cambridge, Massachusetts 02139

Jones, Lew
Coordinator - Information
  Services
SUNY - Oswego
Oswego, New York 13126

Karp, Nancy
Library School Student
University of Michigan
2718 Golfside No. 813
Ann Arbor, Michigan 48104

Kasper, Diane
Reference Librarian
Library
Bowling Green State University
Bowling Green, Ohio 43403

Kelto, Kathy R.
Assistant Reference Librarian
University of Dayton
Dayton, Ohio 45469

Kerns, Ruth
Reference Librarian
Purdue University
Fort Wayne, Indiana 46819

Krueger, Mabre
Head Librarian
Jackson Community College
Jackson, Michigan 49201

Krumins, Sara M.
Reference Librarian
Ferris State College
Big Rapids, Michigan 49307

Kuhtz, Mary Lee
Reference Librarian
Bowling Green State University
Bowling Green, Ohio 43403

LaBue, Benedict
Instructor/Reference Bibliographer
University of Colorado
Boulder, Colorado 80302

Lester, Linda L.
Public Services Librarian
Findlay College
Findlay, Ohio 45840

Lichtenberg, Rita
Assistant Reference Librarian
Indiana University Libraries
Bloomington, Indiana 47401

Liebe, Janice T.
Assistant Librarian
State University College-Brockport
Brockport, New York 14420

Lippincott, Joan K.
Assistant Librarian - Reference
SUNY - Brockport
Brockport, New York 14420

Lonie, Ann
Head, Reference/Bibliographer
Memorial Library
University of Notre Dame
Notre Dame, Indiana 46556

Lutzker, Marilyn
Head, Reader Services
John Jay College of the City
    University of New York
New York, New York 10019

MacDonald, Mary
Instructional Services Librarian
Sangamon State University
Springfield, Illinois 62704

Manley, Nancy
Reserve Book Librarian
Undergraduate Library
University of Illinois
Urbana, Illinois 61801

Mark, Paula F.
Instructional Services Librarian
University of Massachusetts
Amherst, Massachusetts 01002

Mason, Frank
Head, Dental Library
University of Southern California
School of Dentistry
Los Angeles, California 90007

MeriKangas, Robert J.
Assistant Head, Reference Services
University of Maryland
College Park, Maryland 20742

Mertins, Barbara J.
717 South Hills Drive
Morgantown, West Virginia
    26506

Mills, Pam
Technical Services
University of Minnesota
Minneapolis, Minnesota 55455

Mitchell, Doris
Assistant Reference Librarian
Virginia Commonwealth
    University
Richmond, Virginia 23284

Moyer, Sue
Science Librarian
Michigan State University
East Lansing, Michigan 48823

Murray, Raymond
Associate Librarian
SUNY - Oswego
Oswego, New York 13126

Nelson, Barbara
Technical Services Librarian
John Wesley College
Owosso, Michigan 48867

Nelson, Ilene
Assistant Reference Librarian
University of South Carolina
Columbia, South Carolina 29208

Netz, David J.
Director, Learning Resources
Central College
Pella, Iowa 50219

Olson, John
Reference Librarian
Schoolcraft College
Livonia, Michigan 48151

Parker, Diane C.
Head, Reference Department
Lockwood Library
SUNY - Buffalo
Buffalo, New York 14214

Parsons, Linda
Technical Services
University of Minnesota
Minneapolis, Minnesota 55455

Pausch, Lois
Cataloger
University of Illinois
Urbana, Illinois 61801

Peyton, Anne
Media Reserve Advisor
Hampshire College
Amherst, Massachusetts 01002

Phillips, Linda
Librarian
Ohio State University
Agricultural Technical Institute
Wooster, Ohio 44691

Phipps, Shelley E.
Orientation Librarian
University of Arizona
Tucson, Arizona 85706

Plank, Marietta A.
Head, Information/Instruction
    Services
Penn State University
University Park, Pennsylvania 16802

Porter, Margaret L.
Assistant Librarian, Information
    Services
Community College of Allegheny
    County
Pittsburgh, Pennsylvania 15212

Radtke, Eugene
Reference Librarian
Kalamazoo Valley Community
   College
Kalamazoo, Michigan 49009

Reeves, Pamela W.
Associate Librarian
Cuyahoga Community College
Cleveland, Ohio 44115

Reichel, Mary
Education Reference
   Librarian
University of Nebraska -
   Omaha
Box 688
Omaha, Nebraska 68101

Rice, Sheila
Orientation Librarian
Undergraduate Library
University of Michigan
Ann Arbor, Michigan 48104

Richardson, Robert J.
Reference Librarian
Drake Library
SUNY - Brockport
Brockport, New York 14420

Ringland, Inez
Reference Librarian
DePaul University
2323 N. Seminary
Chicago, Illinois 60614

Robertson, Margaret W.
Cataloger
University of Illinois
Urbana, Illinois 61801

Rzasa, Kathryn
Reference Librarian
Texas A &M University
College Station, Texas 77840

Schlauch, Edward
Reference Librarian
S. Samuel Library
University of Toronto
Toronto, Ontario, Canada

Schmitt, Demaris Ann
Reference Librarian
Meramec Community College
Kirkwood, Missouri

Scoll, Del
Washtenaw Community College
Ann Arbor, Michigan 48107

Scott, Consuela
Librarian
West Los Angeles College
Culver City, California 90230

Sharer, Mary Elizabeth
Reference Librarian
Undergraduate Library
University of Maryland
College Park, Maryland 20742

Sharma, Ravindra N.
Reference Librarian
Colgate University
Hamilton, New York 13346

Shaughnessy, Honora Ann
Librarian
EVDS Unit - Library
University of Calgary
2920 24th Avenue, N.W.
Calgary, Alberta
Canada C2N 1N4

Sherrill, Rebecca
Assistant Librarian - Public
   Services
Miami University - Hamilton
Hamilton, Ohio 45011

Sherwood, Virginia
Head, Instructional Services
University of California -
  San Diego
LaJolla, California 92037

Singley, Elijah
Public Services Librarian
Lincoln Land Community
  College
Springfield, Illinois 62708

Slayton, Robert
Head Librarian
Vincennes University
Vincennes, Indiana 47591

Smith, Aline
Reference Librarian
University of Detroit
Detroit, Michigan 48221

Smith, William Todd, Jr.
Art Director/Photographer
Gray & Kilgore, Inc.
Detroit, Michigan 48207

Snarskis, Joyce B.
Assistant Professor
Library Instructional Services
Sangamon State University
Springfield, Illinois 62708

Sparks, Rita
Reference Librarian
Oakland University
Rochester, Michigan 48063

Sternlicht, Dorothy
Associate Librarian
Penfield Library
SUNY-Oswego
Oswego, New York 13126

Stockard, Joan
Readers Services Librarian
Wellesley College
Wellesley, Massachusetts 02181

Stoffle, Carla J.
Head, Public Services Division
University of Wisconsin - Parkside
Kenosha, Wisconsin 53140

Strohl, LeRoy
Librarian
Emory & Henry College
Emory, Virginia 24327

Thielemeir, Mary E.
Media Specialist Librarian
Atlanta Junior College
Atlanta, Georgia 30310

Trezevant, Carolyn
Assistant Reference Librarian
East Texas State University
Commerce, Texas 75428

Trumbore, Jean F.
Associate Reference Librarian
University of Delaware
Newark, Delaware 19711

Tucker, Mark
Reference Librarian
Wabash College
Crawfordsville, Indiana 47933

Wade, Diana M.
Assistant Reference Librarian
University of Illinois Library
Urbana, Illinois 61801

Ward, James E.
Director of the Library
David Lipscomb College
Nashville, Tennessee 37203

Watts, Anne
Librarian II, Reference
University of Missouri
St. Louis, Missouri 63031

Willar, Arline
Assistant Librarian, Public Services
Northeastern University
Boston, Massachusetts 02115

Williams, Maudine B.
Head Librarian
Herron School of Art, IUPUI
1701 North Pennsylvania Street
Indianapolis, Indiana 46202

Wilson, Florence J.
Reference Librarian
George Mason University
Fairfax, Virginia 22030

Wilson, Lucy
Public Services Librarian
Raymond Walters College
Blue Ash, Ohio 45206

Wold, Shelley T.
Instructor, Library Science
University of Arkansas - Little Rock
Little Rock, Arkansas 72204

Young, Marjorie
Assistant Librarian
SUNY - New Paltz
Oneonta, New York 13820

Young, Juana
Head, Circulation Department
University of Arkansas
Fayetteville, Arkansas 72701